Past-into-Present Series

The Middle Classes

W. J. Reader

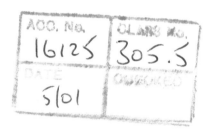

B. T. BATSFORD LTD   London

First published 1972
© W. J. Reader 1972

Filmset by Keyspools Ltd, Golborne, Lancs.

Printed in Great Britain by The Anchor Press Ltd, Tiptree, Essex
for the Publishers
B. T. Batsford Ltd, 4 Fitzhardinge Street, London W1H OAH

ISBN 0 7134 1778 1

Acknowledgments

The author and publishers wish to thank the following for permission to use the illustrations reproduced in this book: Army and Navy Stores Ltd for figs 51, 55; Nick Barrington for fig 4; the BBC for fig 61; British Information Services for fig 64; BUPA for fig 57; Courtaulds Ltd for fig 14; Debenhams Ltd for fig 52; the Department of Defence for fig 24; the GLC for fig 63; Highgate Literary and Scientific Institute Library for fig 25; the Mansell Collection for fig 5; the Nuffield Organisation for fig 54; John Player Ltd for fig 30; Provincial Press Agency for fig 66; Radio Times Hulton Picture Library for figs 20, 43, 47, 59; Eileen Ramsay for fig 65; Douglas Sellick for fig 26; the Stock Exchange for fig 62; Unilever Ltd for fig 31.

Contents

The Illustrations

1 'The Middling Sort of People'

We are quite used to the middle classes nowadays. There they are, wherever you look, in Chairmen's offices, in suburban gardens, in television programmes, in bowler hats, in politics, in righteous indignation. 'Middle class' means ways of earning a living, of dressing, or talking, of going to school, of voting, thinking, holding a knife and fork, and drinking. For some people, the middle classes are 'us': for others – more, no doubt – they are 'them'. For all of us, they are part of the framework of our daily life.

Why?

What made the middle classes?

What, to start with, were they in the middle of?

The short answer is: the Industrial Revolution.

Listen to Sir Charles Trevelyan, who said he belonged to 'a landed country family', speaking in 1857:

> a class between the clergy and the legal and medical professions and the higher merchants on the one side, and the work people on the other . . . the great middle class, who carry on all our great industrial and marine operations.

1 A merchant and his clerk, about 1820. He is probably a ship owner, wealthy and highly respected in some seaport town.

But in 1857 there had not been 'great industrial and marine operations' for very long – operations, that is to say, backed by steam power to drive machinery in factories and to haul railway trains. The beginning of main-line railways, when Trevelyan spoke, was within the grown-up memory of men still in their thirties. Other uses of steam power, especially for pumping mines, went well back into the eighteenth century, but steam had not been widely applied to factory processes until the twenty years or so before Sir Charles's own life-time (he was born in 1807). In 1851, for the first time in any country, more people in Great Britain were reported to be living in towns than in the countryside. In the days before the railways, before the factories, before the large towns, the middle classes were already there, but they were not talked about under that name. They were often called 'the middling sort of people'. Who were they? One answer is that they were the people next below the gentry, which begs the question: who were the gentry? The question is dealt with in another book in this series, and we need do no more, here, than sketch the answer. It lies in Trevelyan's description of himself as belonging to 'a landed country family'. In the days before large-scale industry, land and land alone was the source of wealth, power and social prestige, and the gentry were the land-owners – the owners, that is, of estates large enough to support themselves, their families and their dependants. They did not expect, nor were they expected, to work for their living, but that is not to say that they were idle, for they governed the country, locally and centrally, and they provided officers for the armed forces as well as clergymen for the Church. They had influence in the nation far out of proportion to their numbers. Indeed in a political sense the gentry *were* the nation. Other classes were of small account.

But old English society was not static. The line between the gentry and those immediately below them was thin and frequently crossed in both directions. In land ownership itself there would be little to choose between the large farmer who worked his own land – the yeoman – and the small gentleman who let his estate out to rent. Then estates descended, undivided, from the owner to his eldest son, which meant that younger sons, provided with a little capital from the resources of the estate, must go off and make their own way. This they might do by marrying an heiress or by going into a profession or into a merchant's business, perhaps by marrying a merchant's daughter, and in either of these ways the younger son of a gentleman would enter a middle-class occupation. Successful merchants and professional men, on the other hand, expected to hoist themselves into the ranks of the gentry by buying landed estates and then marrying their children to the heirs and heiresses of other estates, so that within two or three generations all trace of their middle-class origins would be lost, or at least decently hidden.

The representative middle-class man was the merchant – the wholesale trader who lived by buying and selling, and by foreign trade. Merchants would deal in anything saleable – in grain, wool and other farm produce or in such manufactures (literally, hand-made goods) as there were, especially cloth. They would organise production in craftsmen's houses, giving out the raw material, perhaps

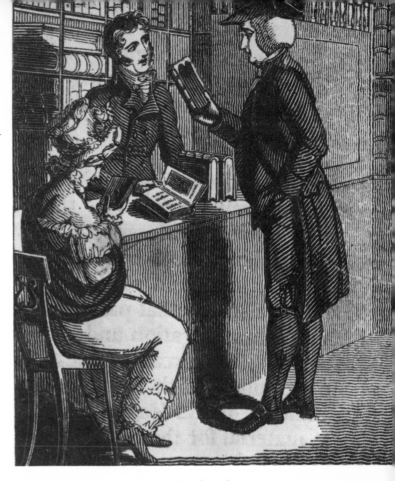

2 A bookseller and his customer, whose hat, clothes and wig show that he is a clergyman, presumably buying some learned work of the classics or theology.

leasing the tools, and buying the finished product but not, as a rule, gathering the craftsmen (the 'manufacturers') under one roof in a 'manufactory'.

The foreign merchants were shipowners. The greatest of them, the 'merchant venturers' of seaport towns, above all London and Bristol, would be very wealthy and very grand indeed, fully able, at the very top, to influence national politics and to look a lord in the eye, or to provide a daughter to marry a lord's son if the nobleman's fortunes were in need of repair.

From these heights the merchants shaded down through such solid citizens as the coal merchants of London and the grain dealers of country towns until they merged with shopkeepers and with the higher branches of handicraft trades – watch-making, instrument-making, tailoring, masonry, joinery – with which shopkeeping had close connections. And there would be masters of industrial processes – millers, smiths, ironfounders – some of whom might carry on their trade remote in woods to provide fuel for smelting, or near a stream to turn a wheel.

Then there were the professional men. By convention there were three 'learned professions', Divinity, Physic and Law. What divided them from meaner occupations was that they required a 'liberal education' – that is, education fit for a member of the governing classes – at a university for clergymen and physicians; at the Inns of Court for lawyers. They were occupations which a gentleman might engage in without disgrace, and if anyone else could scrape into them he could claim to be recognised as a gentleman. Two of them, the Church and the Law, might lead to places of great honour and power. They all had origins running back well into the Middle Ages and they were very different from what is understood by the term 'profession' now. In particular, anyone entering a profession went in first and qualified afterwards, by some form of apprenticeship. The 'liberal education' he was supposed to have had before he entered was supposed to fit him to acquire the professional knowledge he would need. There was no question, in the eighteenth century, of serious qualifying exams, although vestigial remains of oral tests of legal knowledge and of medical knowledge had survived from earlier periods.

The mother of all professions, in a sense, was the Church. In the Middle Ages it had been the home of all learning, and in eighteenth century England it still dominated education. Fellows of colleges in the two universities, Oxford and Cambridge, were nearly all clergymen, and so were nearly all masters in grammar schools. To be a clergyman was natural for a gentleman of intellectual or scientific tastes, and since any gentleman was assumed to be a member of the Church of England, no particular enquiry was made into his religious zeal. He would in any case expect, once ordained, to live the ordinary life of his social equals, taking his place, if his tastes so dictated, on the bench of magistrates or in the hunting field.

Below the 'learned professions' there were other practitioners of the law and of medicine. In the law the higher branch, the barristers, who alone might go on to become judges, were sharply distinguished from the 'attorneys', who did not appear in Court but did all the work necessary to get cases prepared. They also acted in a great deal of other business where legal knowledge was required, particularly the drawing up of wills, the conveyancing of property, mortgaging, leasing, and so on. The attorney was invaluable to the landed gentleman, who referred to him with a good deal of scorn as 'my man of business'. It was a humble occupation, but often lucrative.

In medicine, below the grand and expensive physicians, there were surgeons and apothecaries. The surgeon would no doubt have served an apprenticeship, perhaps in the Navy or the Army, where there was plenty of practice, but he needed no formal qualification before he sawed your leg off without an anaesthetic. The apothecary kept a specialised kind of grocer's shop where he compounded pills and potions. Naturally people came to him for advice, and for a fee he would visit them in their homes, much to the scandal of the physicians. The apothecaries and the surgeons were the ancestors, jointly, of the modern general practitioner, but in the eighteenth century their position was only slightly and precariously higher than that of other handicraftsmen and shopkeepers.

These lower professionals were in fact the men of the future, and we shall meet them again. To the great landowner of the eighteenth century, however, there was hardly anything to choose, socially, between the country doctor or country lawyer and the upper servants – the butler, the steward, the valet, or her ladyship's personal maid. Certainly neither the doctor nor the lawyer would expect

3 Apothecaries were shopkeepers, but they gave medical advice, compounded pills and potions, and visited their wealthier patients. From them and the surgeons the modern family doctor has developed.

(though the parson might) to be entertained as a social equal, and if either called on professional business he would find refreshment, no doubt, in the housekeeper's room. There was a great lady in the eighteenth century, it is said, who would never condescend to address her doctor directly. 'Tell the surgeon,' she would say to a servant in the surgeon's presence, 'he may now bleed the Countess of Carlisle.'

Other professions – architecture, land surveying, civil engineering – were emerging between two and three hundred years ago, and they also found their patrons among the landowners who, apart from the very greatest merchants, were the only masters of property and wealth on anything more than a moderate scale. The Adam brothers built and decorated country mansions, Thomas Chippendale furnished them, 'Capability' Brown laid out their grounds. When the Duke of Bridgewater, who owned coal mines, needed a canal built, he employed James Brindley (1716–1772), once a repairer of old machinery, to do it for him.

The prosperity of the middle classes, before the beginning of modern industry, thus depended very heavily on pleasing those better off and better placed, socially, than themselves: that is, the nobility and gentry. The attorneys looked after their property. The surgeons and apothecaries looked after (or ruined) their health. The shopkeepers sold whatever they needed to buy, especially the luxury goods which their estates would not supply. Corn dealers and wool merchants bought their tenants' produce. Butlers, housekeepers, stewards, ran their immense households. In 1688, the household of a 'temporal lord' (i.e. a lord who was not a bishop) might run to about forty people, as an average; of a 'knight', to thirteen; even of a simple 'gentleman', to eight. At the middle-class level, by contrast, a tradesman's household or a shopkeeper's might average four to five people: even

9

an overseas merchant's, only eight, and that would probably include people working for him in his business.

If the nobility and gentry took their trade away, where could the 'middling sort of people' look for their livelihood? There wasn't much of a living to be made beneath them, for the poor had no property for lawyers to lease, mortgage, devise and entail; no money for doctors' fees; and they depended for clothing, housing and furniture (what little they had) mainly on the discards and throw-outs of the well-to-do. Food of course they must have, but if they couldn't grow or poach it they could only buy very little at a time and that not good.

Probably the first business men to do well out of the lower end of the market were the brewers, beer being almost as much a necessity of life as bread and much more difficult to make at home. It lent itself to large-scale factory production (big brewers were among the earliest users of steam power, after the mine-owners) and great fortunes carried Whitbread, Guinness and others from the middle classes of the eighteenth century towards the nobility and gentry of the nineteenth and twentieth.

The middle classes in old England served a land-owning aristocracy and an overwhelmingly rural population. The middle-class man, however, must be a townsman, as far as his business is concerned, because he lives by trade and trade without towns is inconceivable. This was as true two or three hundred years ago as it is to-day, and only when a merchant or a banker (the early bankers *were* merchants, trading in money as well as goods) had made really great wealth would he cut himself off from his origins and buy an estate, or perhaps marry the heiress to one. If we want to know what middle-class life was like in the eighteenth century or before, it is to the towns we must look.

None of these towns, even London, was really large by the standards we are used to, although London was enormous for that day and by the time the first census was taken, in 1801, it had something like a million inhabitants, if we include all the sprawling town beyond the ancient city walls. Outside London, well into the eighteenth century, eight or ten thousand inhabitants would make a largish town and not many provincial places, until industrial growth began late in the century, would run much beyond ten thousand. Even after the industrial towns began to grow, it was a long time before country towns expanded very much, and the early nineteenth century census reports are full of not over-large villages (to our way of thinking), each with its mayor and corporation, or portreeve and capital burgesses, or mayor and jurats, or whatever the local usage was for the expression of civic dignity.

A good deal less than twenty minutes' walk, in one of these little places, would carry you clean across from open country on one side to open country on the other, and probably not much more in most of the assize towns and cathedral cities which were the regional and county capitals. Even in the centre, the bigger houses would have large gardens round or behind them, and no one was far separated from the land. The typical middle-class man lived over his shop or beside his mill

4 Axbridge, Somerset, a town since Anglo-Saxon times, when there was a mint there. Below and to the left of the church is the market square. The houses along the right-hand side of the main street have long gardens running up the hill. About half-way up the picture, on the left, is a large nineteenth-century workhouse, now a hospital.

or his brewery, his forge or his foundry. Close around, in far less salubrious surroundings – perhaps rows of cottages or the tumbledown wrecks of houses once inhabited by the well-to-do – the prosperous shopkeeper's poorer neighbours lived, but those whom he employed, as apprentices or perhaps as journeymen, would probably live in his own house until they married. In small places, with two or three thousand inhabitants, the social classes lived intermingled, as later they did not, and it would not be far from the truth to say that everyone knew everyone else, though that is far from saying that they liked each other.

Most towns in the eighteenth century had a free grammar school, generally with one smallish schoolroom and one master, invariably a parson, who might have one assistant. The school would have been endowed by some local worthy, probably a hundred years or so earlier, to educate a dozen or twenty boys without charge to their parents and to send some of them on to Oxford or Cambridge on scholarships provided for the purpose. Some schools admitted girls but not, evidently, the one

John Hughes.

MORDEN HALL
Boarding School, Surrey,
FOR
YOUNG GENTLEMEN.

5 A private boarding school, probably aimed at parents not wealthy enough to afford the public schools. The subjects taught would include a great deal of arithmetic and writing, to enable boys to take jobs as clerks, if they could find them.

which still stands in the Berkshire village of Uffington, founded before 1617 by Thomas Saunders, whose will reads:

> Whereas it is a most common and usual course for many to send their Daughters to common Schools to be taught together with and corrupt all sorts of Youths which course is by many conceived very uncomely and not decent – therefore the said School Master may not admit any of that Sex to be taught in the said School.

These grammar schools gave quite poor boys the opportunity of acquiring both the education and the contacts on which to found a career. Charles Abbott (1762–1832), second son of a Canterbury hairdresser and wigmaker, went on an exhibition from Canterbury Grammar School to Christ Church, Oxford, became a lawyer and, as Lord Tenterden, Chief Justice of the King's Bench. This was an exceptional career, but it illustrates the point that neither the schools nor the universities of eighteenth century England were reserved for the rich.

Eighteenth century England had, in fact, an open society. The class structure was rigid but there was nothing to prevent anyone climbing up through it if he had enough ability, determination (not to say ruthlessness) and luck. Legal obstacles which got in the rising man's way in France and other continental countries did not exist in England – hence the success stories, social as well as financial, of the great brewing families, of several early engineers, of Wedgwood the potter, of Dr Johnson, of various eminent surgeons, and of many others. The way was not easy, but it was there, and although success on the greatest scale was rare, as it always must be, yet the odds against reasonable prosperity, even from very unpromising beginnings, were not impossibly high.

As well as schools, eighteenth century towns usually had some provision for the other end of life, old age. On a board in the parish church, which may still exist,

6 Lord Chief Justice Tenterden, the barber's boy, presented as an example to Victorian working men in a temperance magazine of 1860.

there would be records of property, usually land, left to provide sums of money to be doled out, either in cash or as bread, clothing or coals, to 'the poor of the parish' – or some specified group of them – 'once a year for ever'. Not many towns, either, were without almshouses, though of those which survive there are not many with quite such self-congratulatory inscriptions as, on a sailors' almshouse in Bristol, this:

> Freed from all storms the tempest and the rage
> Of billows here we spend our age.
> Our weather-beaten vessels here repair
> And from the Merchants' kind and generous care
> Find harbour here: no more we put to sea
> Until we launch into Eternity.
>
> And lest our Widows whom we leave behind
> Should want relief they too a shelter find
> Thus all our anxious cares and sorrows cease
> Whilst our kind Guardians turn our toil to ease.
> May they be with an endless Sabbath blest
> Who have afforded unto us this rest.

What more touching tribute to the charity of the middle classes of Bristol could the middle classes of Bristol possibly devise? It would be ungracious, no doubt, to point out that in 1688, which is about the date of this inscription, 'common seamen' who were not being looked after in old age by kind and generous merchants had about £20 a year each to keep their families on, which even in 1688 was not enough.

At the moment of writing it is still possible, though with the present rate of rebuilding it may not be possible for much longer, to see old corporate towns much as they were a couple of hundred years ago. Some, like Axbridge and Wells in Somerset, are almost complete and may not even greatly have outgrown their ancient area. In others it is still possible to see the old centre engulfed in more modern surroundings. In many parish churches there are monuments to bygone burgesses, surgeons, attorneys, schoolmasters, shopkeepers and the like, sometimes showing the civic offices they held and the dates they held them. Some show long family continuity, like the large table tomb in the church at New Romney which commemorates 'Richard Stuppenye jurate of this towne in the first yeare of K. H^y viij who died in the xviij yeare of the saide kynges reigne of whose memorye Clement Stuppenye of the same port his great grandsonne hath caused this tombe to be new erected for the use of the auncient meeting and election of maior and jurats of this port towne june the 10th Anno dm 1622.' The inscription, besides testifying to family piety over four generations, shows an unexpected use for table tombs and calls to mind, by association of ideas, the monument in Chester which

7 Monument to the builder of St. Paul's Cathedral, London, who died in 1723. 'In piety to his GOD, in justice, fidelity, kindness and charity to his neighbour; in temperance, humility, contempt of the world, and the due government of all his appetites and passions; in conjugal and paternal affection; in every relation, every action and scene of life, he was what the best man, the best Christian, would desire to be at the hour of death.'

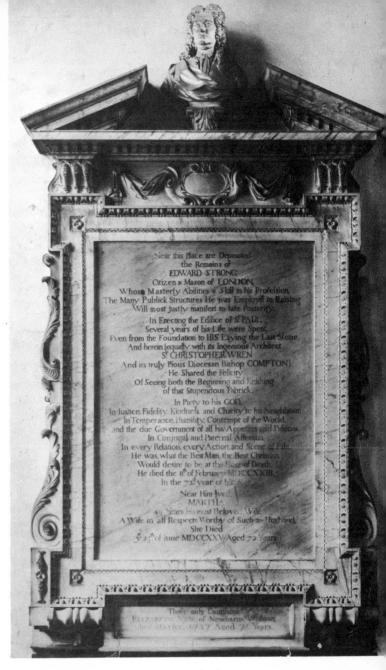

marks the spot where formerly they held 'the annual mayor-making and riot'.

Well, perhaps a riot once a year, and occasional bear-baiting or football in between – they all amounted to much the same thing – would keep the lower orders happy. But this was hardly fitting behaviour for worthy burgesses, with their solid, handsome houses, their charitable bequests, their strong sense of civic dignity, who already by the eighteenth century had a long tradition of a way of life which marked them off, not only from the artisans and poor beneath them, but also, and also with a certain sense of superiority, from the gentry above. Theirs was essentially the way of life of a class in which every man had his way to make and was encouraged to push his abilities to the uttermost, without being able to rely, as the gentleman could, on the strength of an established position; and of a class for which the possibility of ruin, of a calamitous descent from comfort into destitution, was too real and too close to be ignored. The Bristol merchant might look after his ancient mariners with a good deal of condescension, but he knew very well that he might suffer shipwreck as well as they.

These circumstances produced devotion to sober, regular conduct, to hard work, to very careful and far-sighted use of money, partly to build prosperity during the working years, partly to provide security against old age, partly to launch children, particularly sons, into the same strenuous world. These were not qualities admired by the gentry, whose social position was secure and who took money for granted, so that they used it for display rather than investment and guided their conduct by rules of honour, essentially military, rather than by rules of prudence, essentially commercial. At the other end of the scale the artisan or labourer was inclined to use money, when he had any, for immediate enjoyment as long as it lasted, without much thought of what might happen after, either to him or his family. Hence the despairing complaints of James Watt and others, when factory industry was just coming in, that they could never, or hardly ever, find steady workmen. Even the best mechanics and craftsmen, after working very hard for a spell, would take their money and disappear for several days' drinking, and

8 From *Punch*, 1855. 'Mr. Hall, Chief Magistrate at Bow Street, cannot discover any "inconvenience" in the present working of the Act, but recommends that the poor Sunday excursionist should "strap a knapsack on his back, with two or three bottles, and the child to boot, sooner than that Sunday should be desecrated by opening the public-house".'

then come back to earn some money to do the same again. Very well, but that was no way for a sober Scottish engineer to keep a pumping engine going.

Two or three generations back, many eighteenth century shopkeepers and merchants must have had Puritan ancestors – some of them, no doubt, in arms against the King. In quieter times, it was still from the middle classes that Nonconformity drew most of its support, so that in another street from the parish church there would be the Independent (Congregational) chapel, and perhaps a Quaker meeting house somewhere else again. Sober, serious, God-fearing, the middle classes preserved English Puritanism intact throughout the eighteenth century, to come to the surface of affairs again, again linked with radical politics, in the nineteenth.

FURTHER READING

Charles Wilson, *England's Apprenticeship 1603–1763*, 1965.
Dorothy Marshall, *English People in the Eighteenth Century*, 1956.
R. Robson, *The Attorney in Eighteenth-Century England*, 1959.
Tobias Smollett, *Humphrey Clinker*, Everyman edition.
Elizabeth Gaskell, *Wives and Daughters*, Penguin edition.
George Eliot, *Middlemarch*, Penguin edition.

2 'The Great Middle Class'

He that would thrive
Must rise at five.
He that hath thriven
May lie till seven.
                    Traditional (18th century ?).

In 1800 Great Britain was about to lead the rest of the world into the greatest change in the way people live since the New Stone Age, and much the fastest change, of its kind and scope, in human history. In 1800 British society, like civilised society everywhere else, was based almost entirely on agriculture, but already power-driven cotton mills were widespread in Lancashire and already several engineers had conceived the idea of making steam power drive ships and loco-motives. By 1851, with more people living in towns than out of them, with a comprehensive system of main-line railways, with steam ships at sea, and with steam power driving all kinds of factory machinery, the decisive changeover had been made. It was far from complete, it is still not complete, and no one could say then or can say now where or how far it would go but in the first fifty years of the nineteenth century, in Great Britain, a very long step was taken in the most funda-mental advance in man's control over his environment since, in the unrecorded depths of prehistory, hunting gave way to agriculture.

Why this change came about, why it started in Great Britain, are questions too large to be dealt with here. The point that directly interests us is that somewhere very near the centre of the change were the British middle classes. Energetic, self-confident, ambitious, they needed only opportunity. Now it came. From being merely 'the middling sort of people' they could grow into 'the great middle class'.

This transformation did not come from the ownership of wealth – the middle classes, even at the top, were never anywhere near so rich as the great landowners – but from having the skill and the nerve to put it to productive use. Money could be used to buy land and build great houses, but in that case it would only grow slowly, if it grew at all, and it might disappear altogether ('fools build for wise men to live in'). The middle classes used money to build factories and equip them; to build ships and finance their voyages; to build canals and railways; to back inventors in the hope, often vain, that they might eventually make money. These activities could lose money, and frequently did, but if they were successful they would produce profits which could be put back into the business or lent to other people to develop their businesses. It was a risky way of making a living, but it was part of the middle class way of life and it could be immensely rewarding, both for

9 Messrs. Marshall's Flax Mill, Leeds. An unusually large factory building of the 1860s. The building on the left is the office block, built in Egyptian style after a design by the sculptor Joseph Bonomi. The mill chimney was to represent an obelisk and the roof to be turfed for grazing sheep.

10 *Great Eastern*, designed by I. K. Brunel (1806–1859), launched 1858, broken up 1888. At 32,000 tons displacement, much the largest ship in the world until the early years of the twentieth century.

11 George Stephenson (1781–1848), railway engineer. 'The time will come when it will be cheaper for a working man to make a journey by railway than to walk on foot.'

the individual investor and for the community at large. As the pace of economic development quickened, from the late eighteenth century on, there were more and more opportunities for investment on a greater and greater scale. Private capitalism began to show its power as an agent of economic growth.

The transformation of England into an industrial country required more than shrewd investment. It required human energy, energy fierce and acquisitive, energy physical and creative, energy poured out at high pressure and sustained for the better part of two generations – that is, for the first half of the nineteenth century. This also the middle classes could supply. Hard work, for themselves and others, had all the force of their dour religion behind it to reinforce earthbound motives, and as well as hard work they produced organising ability and technical virtuosity necessary for industrial growth on a scale never seen in the world before.

This roaring, scrambling energy put up the cotton mills, the blast furnaces, the engineering shops, the new industrial towns – sprawling, insanitary, full of violence, yet the source of wealth much more widely distributed than ever before. The energy of the early nineteenth century produced also the world's first trunk railway system – 5,000 miles of it built by manual labour in well under twenty years under the impetus of men like I. K. Brunel, who as well as getting the Great Western Railway built also designed the largest and most advanced steamships of his day (*Great Western*, 1837; *Great Britain*, 1843; *Great Eastern*, 1858), designed numerous bridges, and succeeded in getting trains to go by the pressure of the atmosphere behind them.

By effort on this scale and of this intensity Great Britain managed to sustain, more or less, a population which almost doubled between 1801 and 1851 (10,690,000 to 20,880,000). In this population there was a great deal of poverty, as people at the time knew very well. What gave them hope was that by the mid-century there was evidence that the new industrial society was beginning to provide a standard of life, for the mass of the population, far higher than anything that was possible in a purely agricultural society.

The usual method of raising capital in Victorian England was through family and friends. Bankers did not consider it part of their job to provide long-term finance and individuals, for obvious reasons, did not lend readily unless they knew the borrowers well. Starting capital, therefore, usually came from relations, close friends, or business associates. If the business prospered, the owners, when they needed fresh capital, would wish to oblige their friends and they would also not wish to lose control to strangers, so that once again they would probably go to people well-known to them, not to strangers. Throughout the nineteenth century, and in many industries for far longer, the basic operating unit in British business was the family firm, belonging either to one family or to the families of two or more partners.

Family businesses, like the family estates of the gentry, were expected to provide a continuing source of livelihood for the owners. They expected sons, sons-in-law and nephews to follow them. Only in very exceptional, often desperate, circumstances would they bring outsiders into the management. In any appointment from beyond the family circle, preference would usually be given to friends or sons of friends, rather than to strangers. Nobody would be likely to consider this

12 Thomas Coutts (1735–1822), banker. Co-founder of Coutts & Co., London. 'He was a gentleman of wide accomplishments' – he married for the second time at the age of eighty – 'and very charitable. While admitted into the highest circles, he was of economical habits, and amassed a fortune to the value of about £900,000.'

reprehensible – indeed, much the reverse, for a man had a duty to his family and friends – unless it was obvious that people who were manifestly incompetent were being appointed. But this was not very likely, for the owners would have close personal knowledge of the people they took on, very important when the prosperity of the firm would depend on the wisdom of their choice. They might make mistakes, but on the whole it seems doubtful whether anyone has yet developed any better system of management selection than shrewd nepotism.

Family firms in the early nineteenth century were private partnerships, in which each partner might be held liable for the whole of the firm's debts. Towards the end of the century, after changes in the law, the larger and more successful businesses were mostly turned into limited companies, in which shareholders' liability was limited to the extent of their holdings. This meant that members of the family not actively employed in the business – unmarried daughters, maiden aunts, sons who had improved the family's social standing by going into the Army – could safely be provided for. It also made the raising of fresh capital easier, because outside investors could be offered preference shares while the ordinary shares, carrying control of the company, remained with the original owners. By a device of this kind W. H. Lever, the founder of Lever Brothers Limited, kept control until well into the twentieth century of a world-wide group of companies with capital employed of about £60m.

In Great Britain, until long after the mid-nineteenth century, there were not many really large undertakings except three or four of the biggest railway companies, which were in a class of their own. In the traditional middle-class businesses of wholesale and retail trade, or in services like banking and insurance, the

13 A family business.

52, REGENT STREET.

RETIRING FROM BUSINESS.

Mr. DEBENHAM, Sen., after a prolonged but successful battle with the world for fifty years, has resolved, on the Anniversary of his Business Career, the 13th February, to retire in favour of his Sons.

really large organisation or the really large shop – the department store – with clerks or assistants in hundreds, hardly began to come into existence until late in the century. In manufacturing industry mass production, in anything like its modern form, was unknown until, again towards the end of the century, it began to come in for some kinds of consumer goods, especially soap. In engineering, metalwork, the pottery trades, and over a wide range of other activities factory work in 1850 was a matter for skilled craftsmen working partly with machine tools but also, very largely, by hand, and the traditions of that kind of work have lingered up to the present day, especially in shipbuilding, in a multiplicity of craft unions. Mining was entirely a manual operation, sometimes assisted by explosives, throughout the nineteenth century, and house-building has barely become a factory industry yet.

Most owners of factories, under these conditions, were not large employers. An attempt was made at the mid-century Census – 1851 – to find out how many 'masters in trades' there were and how many people each of them employed. The results, which were admitted to be incomplete, suggested that of about 130,000 'masters' in England and Wales, nearly 90,000 employed eight or nine men each, on average, and that only 752 employed 150 men or more. Other evidence, from the records of individual firms, suggests that at this time a business with 1,000 or

14 Samuel Courtauld (1793–1881). His firm prospered on Victorian mourning crepe; later on rayon. It became a public company in 1904, and is today capitalised at more than £500m.

more employees, like Courtaulds' silk business in Essex, would be very large indeed; that an engineering firm with 600 men or so, like Fairbairns at Leeds, would be large; and that a labour force of 200 to 300, in most industries, would represent a bigger firm than most.

Below that level, numbers would tail away down to threes and fours and half-dozens working in appalling conditions in backstreet workshops – match-making perhaps, or tailoring, or metal-working in Birmingham – and to 'masters' working on their own, indistinguishable in upbringing, family background and general circumstances from the rest of the working-class population around them. The smallest employers were generally the worst, because the small man would be placed so precariously himself that he could not afford decent working conditions or decent wages. A trade union campaign of arson, bombing and shooting (fortunately the pistols were home-made and very bad) against unpopular brick-makers near Manchester, in the late eighteen-fifties and early sixties, was directed entirely against very small employers on much the same social level as the men, to whom some of them were related.

Alongside the business men of the early nineteenth century, professional men were rising also. The attorneys, since the late eighteenth century, had been trying to assert something like equality with the barristers: the surgeons and apothecaries, with the physicians. The Bar, leading to the Bench, was long established as a trade for gentlemen: gentlemen might also be physicians, though rather more recently and more doubtfully, but both barristers and physicians, in general esteem and social standing, far outranked the despised attorneys, the bloodstained surgeons, the shopkeeping apothecaries. This was a state of affairs which the practitioners of the 'lower branches' were determined to change, but they were intelligent enough to see that society would not respect them unless they were respectable, both in professional education and in professional ethics. Once they could show that they really had expert knowledge and that they were unlikely to cheat their clients, then they might hope to improve their social standing – and their fees. More, they might be able to persuade Parliament to grant them monopoly rights in the practice of their professions.

In the late eighteenth and early nineteenth centuries a powerful movement developed for improving professional education, for enforcing adequate standards of qualification and for eliminating disreputable and unqualified practitioners. Pressure was pumped up by the growing demand for professional services which the general development of the nation's business brought with it. If partnerships were being formed, lawyers must draw up the deeds. If more people were growing rich, more people would be able to pay more – and, they hoped, better – doctors to look after them. If the well-to-do were building houses, they would need architects to design them, and of course as they acquired property they would acquire the old upper-class pre-occupation with its administration and disposal. Probably the greatest stimulus of all came from the development of railways in the eighteen-forties. They needed engineers both mechanical and civil; land surveyors; law-

15 A group of Victorian engineers with the Britannia bridge (opened 1850) in the background, uncompleted. The bridge was designed by Robert Stephenson (1803–1859), son of George Stephenson.

yers – never had there been such a feast for lawyers as the railways provided in property transactions and in Parliamentary work – and the very large railway financial affairs demanded accountants rather than simply book-keepers.

In these conditions the modern idea of professional standing took shape. In the old days, although the professions were called 'learned', such training as there was was carried out mostly on the job, in the ancient traditions of craft apprenticeship. The practitioner qualified by experience and his 'learning' was tested only by the most perfunctory exams, or by none at all. The reformers fought to get a profession recognised as an occupation requiring a high standard of training, preferably reinforced by liberal education, and a professional man as one whose knowledge of his calling had been tested by written and oral examination. Practitioners who qualified in this way, through long and presumably arduous training, claimed that they had earned a right to some kind of protection against unqualified competition – protection which, they said, would be to the public advantage as much as their own – but they often found it difficult to get Parliament, which did not like monopolies, to see their point of view. In return for their privileged position, professional men claimed to observe a code of conduct which avoided the baser arts of commercialism, including advertising and price competition, and recognised a duty to the client and to the public which went beyond the not over-refined morality of Victorian business practice.

The fight for improved professional standing was led by attorneys in the law and by general practitioners – surgeons and apothecaries – in medicine. Both had to overcome vested interests in the higher branches of their own professions as well as opponents outside it. The attorneys, discreet and usually decorous in their dealings with the Bar, had their own governing body, the Law Society, by 1825 and written qualifying examinations by 1836. The doctors, by contrast, were noisy, quarrelsome, and split into innumerable factions, so that the Medical Act of 1858, which gave the profession the outline of its present legal framework, was the seventeenth in a succession of Bills presented to Parliament from 1840 on. The first sixteen were all wrecked, partly by the opposition of interests outside the profession, partly by the chances of party politics, and partly by the internal quarrels of the doctors amongst themselves.

Where lawyers and doctors led, engineers, architects, pharmacists, dentists, vets, surveyors, accountants and others could follow. By the third quarter of the century the procedure was pretty well understood for turning a trade into a profession. A professional association should be established by Royal Charter and qualification by written examination should be made compulsory, though on

16 London's first railway, opened from London Bridge to Deptford in 1836, and to Greenwich in 1838. The engineer, Col. G. T. Landmann, R.E. (1779–1854), (fourth from left), is receiving the Lord Mayor.

this point the barristers and the civil engineers were sceptical and dilatory. The barristers thought that although knowledge of the law might be indispensable for attorneys it was far less necessary for them. What the barrister needed was the advocate's ability to persuade judge and jury, and how could you test that except in Court? 'If a man be not competent,' as one eminent QC put it in 1854, 'he will never succeed at the Bar; and if he be, he ought not to be excluded' – that is, by failing an exam. Grumbling, the barristers made examinations compulsory (but simple) in 1872. The civil engineers, deeply suspicious of book learning, held out against compulsory examination until 1898, and other engineers even longer.

The final recognition of professional standing, by no means always achieved, was to get an Act of Parliament making unqualified practice difficult or, preferably, illegal. The doctors, who had so much to do with the development of professional standing, did not get quite all they wanted. The Medical Act of 1858 set up a register of medical practitioners to which no one could be admitted who had not qualified by examination, and registration conferred important rights, especially in signing death certificates and in prescribing dangerous drugs. To the doctors' disgust, however, unqualified practice was not specifically forbidden, and to this day anyone can set up in any branch of medical practice without qualifications of any kind without breaking the law unless he does those things which only registered medical practitioners are permitted to do. Over the whole range of professional activities, and not only in medicine, Parliament has always been unwilling to grant monopolies, partly to avoid interfering too much with the freedom of action of aspiring practitioners, partly to preserve the freedom of choice of intending clients, and partly because unqualified people, highly uncongenial to the established members of a profession, sometimes have good ideas it would be a pity to strangle at birth.

The idea of 'professional standing', as it developed in the nineteenth century, is one of the subtlest conceptions of the middle-class mind. On the one hand, it embraces thoroughly earthy ideas of job protection, job demarcation, and 'the rate for the job' which are also part of the conventional wisdom of trade unions. On the other hand it promotes devotion not only to good workmanship but to something more: sound education at the highest level and the advancement of knowledge. Moreover a professional man knows that he is required to respect, sometimes at his own expense, both the interest of his client and the public interest. The two can sometimes conflict, and then it seems that the client's interest ought to prevail, with results which may be painful for the professional man in the case.

The professional man is at all times in business, selling services backed by specialised knowledge, skill and experience, which keeps him firmly in the middle-class tradition of trade. If he works with his hands, as surgeons and dentists do, he has affinities also with the skilled craftsman. To all this he adds, or should add, respect for knowledge, truth and integrity which set him at the highest level of the trading community, if not apart from them altogether. In addition he can usually earn a very good income, and this was especially true in the nineteenth century.

27

He thus combines in his own person all the most desirable attributes of the trading middle class with qualities which give him a claim to rank as a gentleman. 'The importance of the professions, and the professional classes can scarcely be over-rated,' wrote a barrister in 1857, 'they form the head of the great English middle class, maintain its tone of independence, keep up to the mark its standard of morality, and direct its intelligence.'

By the time those words were written, the middle classes were in full flower, with two main branches and innumerable twigs, some upper, some lower. One main branch, running back to the ancient trading stock of medieval merchants and shopkeepers, was by now in luxuriant bloom with the business men, manufacturers and others, of the Industrial Revolution. There was this branch's finely cultivated offshoot, the new professional class, sharing the same tough and knotty roots yet pointing upward towards the sunshine of gentility. On these two groups, the business men and the professional men, the well-being of the nation now overwhelmingly depended, and they knew it. The 'great English middle class' had developed economic, social and political horsepower such as the 'middling sort of people' had never possessed. We must see what use they made of it.

FURTHER READING

E. J. Hobsbawm, *Industry and Empire*, an economic history of Britain since 1750, 1968.

Peter Mathias, *The First Industrial Nation*, an economic history of Britain 1700–1914, 1969.

S. G. Checkland, *The Rise of Industrial Society in England 1815–1885*, 1964.

Harold Perkin, *The Origins of modern English Society 1780–1880*, 1969.

Samuel Smiles, *Self Help*, intro. by Asa Briggs, 1958.

Great Exhibition Catalogue, reprinted (in part) as *Great Exhibition, London 1851* by David & Charles, 1970.

Punch, bound volumes.

3 The Take-Over Bid

I work at business because business is life. It enables me to do things.

Lord Leverhulme (1851–1925)

Middle-class men, with their self-confidence (sometimes including self-righteousness), personal ambition and urgent thrust toward better things, are often revolutionaries. Indeed it seems to be pretty near the truth to say that a revolution is unlikely to succeed without middle-class leadership. Peasants' revolts and the like, including working-class revolts in early nineteenth century England, have usually been incompetently run and have often been bloodily repressed. The leaders of the highly successful French and Russian revolutions, on the other hand, to say nothing of nationalist successors to British imperialism, most of them from middle-class backgrounds and often expensively educated, have been able to organise the bloody repression of their opponents.

17 From the *British Workman*, 1856.

Plenty of revolutionary fuel was lying about in early nineteenth century England. Economic dislocation caused by the long French wars and by some manifestations of industrialisation produced horrible social conditions amongst the poor in town and country, so that plenty of men were desperate enough for any kind of violence. Violence, in the first forty years or so of the century, kept on breaking out, but in the form of ill-planned and unsustainable riots and terrorism rather than as a really formidable revolutionary campaign. With competent middle-class leadership matters might have been different, but no such leadership appeared. Why not? The answer is not that the middle classes were smugly content with things as they were. They would have been blind to their own interest if they had been, and that is not what they have usually been accused of. They were determined, on the contrary, to make great changes in the national way of life, but not by destroying the system. What middle-class reformers of the early nineteenth century set out to do was to take the system over and re-fashion it so that it would operate both as they thought it ought to, morally, and to their own practical advantage. If the system could be made to operate to the advantage of the middle classes, who could deny that the nation as a whole would have a great deal of good done to it? As Richard Cobden once observed to the House of Commons: 'If you

18 'Enthusiasm displayed'. George Whitfield (1714–1770), an early Methodist, preaching. 'Enthusiasm' in the eighteenth century meant fanaticism: the word is not intended as a compliment.

talk of your aristocracy and your traditions, and compel me to talk of the middle and industrious classes, I say it is to them that the glory of this country is owing.'

The middle-class take-over bid for the leadership of British society – it was nothing less – began, characteristically, with a thorough-going attempt to cleanse the moral tone of the nation. That meant chiefly the moral tone of the other classes in society, upper and lower. The middle classes themselves needed comparatively little cleansing, and such as they did need was administered to them by Rev. John Wesley and his associates from about 1740 on. By the seventeen-eighties the new Puritanism was a rapidly growing force, linked not only with religion but with the movement to clean up corruption in public life and to reform Parliament – a movement which had the hearty goodwill of the middle classes, who profited very little from the patronage associated with the old Parliamentary system. In religious matters, the new ideas were associated not only with the Methodists but with a group in the Church of England (which John Wesley claimed never to have left) who came to be known as Evangelicals.

Amongst the upper classes of eighteenth century England there was an easy-going, sceptical attitude towards religion which was quite at odds with the serious-minded, perhaps also narrow-minded, views of the heirs of the Puritans. Indeed in good society anything in the nature of religious zeal was strongly disapproved of. 'Pious without Enthusiasm' says an eighteenth century lady's epitaph in Gloucester Cathedral, and that was intended as a high compliment.

This coolness toward religion, going so far in some minds as free-thinking and even atheism, though neither were respectable, went with a style of life which to

19 Two sides of a medal commemorating a Sunday School founded at Stockport in 1805. There was very little opportunity for 'the children of the labouring poor' to go to school except on Sundays.

the Methodist or Evangelical observer appeared regrettably frivolous. The upper classes enjoyed, amongst other things, horse-racing, gambling, drinking, the theatre, dancing and pretty women. They seemed to have no sense of sin, even when they went to parties on Sundays. And they fought duels. Altogether neither the religious and intellectual temper of the nobility and gentry nor the way in which they were seen or reported (and reports would lose nothing in the telling) to pass their time were such as to commend themselves to earnest minds in Manchester, nor for that matter in the City of London, which had a long Puritan and radical tradition behind it.

If the view upwards from a middle-class standpoint was unedifying, downwards the view was even worse. The lower orders seemed to have no religion and no sense of responsibility at all. They must be brought to proper habits of industry and thrift, to dutiful respect and gratitude to their superiors, especially their employers, and, of course, to a sense of sin. What, therefore, more fitting than that in Stockport near Manchester, in 1805, there should be erected, by voluntary subscription, a four-storey Sunday school 'for the education and religious instruction of the children of the labouring poor'? Having put up the school, the trustees commemorated it by striking handsome silver medals, and presented themselves with one each.

So long as the old order lasted, with the landed families firmly in control, there was not much likelihood of the middle class leading the rest of the nation towards accepting their own version of the good life. Gentlemen, generally speaking, abominated Wesley and all his works, and they were not likely to change their minds because shopkeepers thought they ought to.

Towards the end of the eighteenth century, nevertheless, matters began to change. A trend set in, high in society, towards much greater strictness and much less permissiveness than the upper classes had been used to since Charles II came back. Among the leaders of the new, or revived, way of life many of the most prominent – William Wilberforce, Hannah More, Henry Thornton – had strong middle-class links, and although they moved in much higher circles the tendency of their influence was towards a way of life which many middle-class people, since the seventeenth century and before, had never wholly ceased to believe in and to practice.

The new puritans, like the old, disapproved of gambling, of heavy drinking, of 'strong language', of dancing and the theatre. They insisted on rigid Sunday observance, based on the Jewish law of the Sabbath rather than on the Christian precept: 'The Sabbath is made for man, not man for the Sabbath.' Their views on sexual morality, especially for women, caused them to draw curtains of obscurity and disapproval across the whole of 'that sort of thing', much to the astonishment of old ladies who had been accustomed to a good deal of freedom both in conversation and behaviour. Young men who held views of this sort went out of their way to scandalize their elders with the shortness of their hair, and then held forth on their elders' regrettable lack of moral fibre.

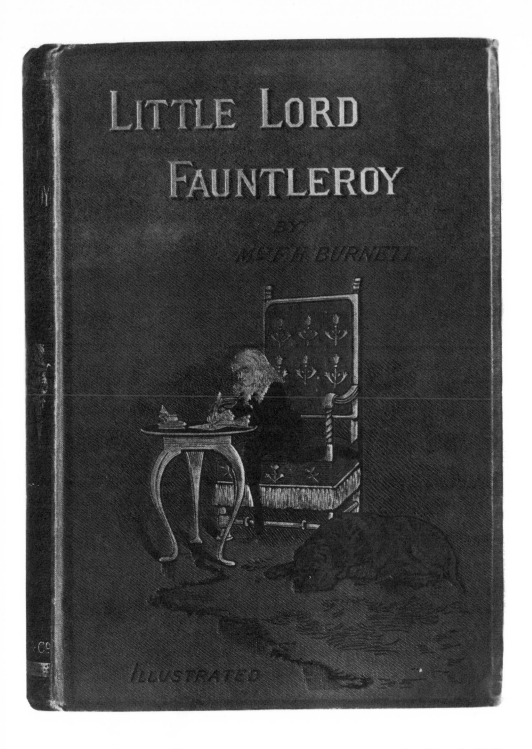

20 A famous (and improving) Victorian childrens' story about an American boy who is discovered to be the heir to an English peerage.

The ungentlemanly ideas of the new fanatics might do very well for the lower classes, and if they were linked to proper respect for social superiors they might help to combat the odious Jacobin notions which began to come over from France in the seventeen-nineties. For this practical reason, if for no other, evangelical principles found support among the rulers of the nation, whether they regulated their own conduct by them or not. There were at all times noble eccentrics who were prepared to do so. One was the first Earl of Egmont (1683–1748), whose son added to the family reputation for oddity by building Enmore Castle in Somerset with medieval fortifications, against the day when firearms should be abolished and decency restored to warfare. Selina Countess of Huntingdon (1707–1791) was a patroness of early Methodism and foundress of 'Lady Huntingdon's Connexion', a new sect. As a third, perhaps, one might name King George III although, as a Hanoverian, he was only rather dubiously an English gentleman.

On the whole, the new Puritanism was stoutly resisted in high society and it was never entirely successful there. Victorian worthies, if that is the right word, like Wellington, Palmerston and Albert Edward, Prince of Wales, continued in an older tradition of royal and noble behaviour, and in Victorian fiction shocking but delightful baronets continued to show what the lower orders believed, not without a degree of truth, about the morals of the gentry.

What is remarkable is not that individuals in high society went on behaving as individuals in high society always had behaved. That was to be expected. The remarkable thing is that by the mid-century the new, or revived, ideas of proper behaviour had made such progress and were so vehemently supported by public opinion that the nobility and gentry were conventionally expected to subscribe to them. For the first time in English history those at the top had been obliged to accept, outwardly at least, a moral code which to a large degree had been pushed up at them from below.

It was not enough to get the nobility and gentry to behave themselves. Their privileged position must also be opened to middle-class penetration. In political terms that meant an assault on the unreformed Parliament and on the Corn Laws, each of which symbolised the predominance of the landed interest over the interest of trade and industry. In the drive for parliamentary reform, which came close to producing a revolutionary situation in the early eighteen-thirties, the middle classes had a good deal of support from below, among working-class Chartists, but in the campaign against the Corn Laws, ten years or so later, the classes began to part company. Chartism in the forties, when there was great distress among the poor, became more and more a working-class movement with which Cobden, Bright and the other middle-class leaders of the repeal campaign were totally out of sympathy.

By the mid-forties the middle classes had won their major political battles. The Reform Act of 1832 had recognised their new political weight (while conceding no weight at all to the working classes) and the campaign against the Corn Laws had shown how they could use it, powerfully aided by two very middle-class institutions: the new railway system and the penny post. Having made their political points, the middle classes were content to leave the traditional governing classes in power, since it was quite certain that any attempt to use power against the general middle class interest could be defeated, and if necessary enough pressure could be generated, as it had been by the Anti Corn Law League, to push through any measure which the middle classes as a whole supported. Politics for their own sake did not interest the middle classes very much, and on these terms most middle-class men were quite happy to leave government to their betters, since it seemed to interest them, and to get on with the things the middle classes really cared about.

Among these, secure and lucrative employment came at the head of the list. In spite of their general expansiveness and prosperity, the Victorian middle classes were plagued by a shortage of good jobs for their sons. This was largely because, as we have already noticed, Victorian business was not in general conducted on a large enough scale to provide much in the way of good salaried employment. If you belonged to an owning family, very well: a position would be found for you if at all possible, though even then it might not be possible to fit in all the sons. If you had capital, you could set up for yourself in business or a profession. If you had to look for a job, the prospect was not hopeful. When Nobel's Explosives Company of Glasgow, in 1880, advertised for an assistant to the general manager, they had nearly 400 applicants to choose from. A man might work all his life as a clerk, thinking himself fortunate to have 'a situation', and he would be quite highly paid if he got £200 a year, with no hope of a retirement pension unless his employer was charitably disposed.

21 The raggedness of these lawyers' clerks suggests the shortage of good salaried employment for the Victorian middle classes. Their client (seated on the left) seems to be an army officer, perhaps seeking the attorney's advice on raising money.

22 A cartoon from *Punch*, 1855:
'*Youthful Swell:* Now Charley – you're just in time for breakfast – have a cup of coffee.
Languid Swell (probably in government office): Thanks! No! If I was to take a cup of coffee in the morning it would keep me awake all day!'

In Victorian England much the largest employer of salaried staff – indeed, almost the only really large one, after the end of the East India Company – was the Government. Officers had to be found for the Army and Navy; clerks for the civil service. The numbers ran into thousands, whereas not even the largest private employers, except perhaps the largest railways, were likely to be able to provide comparable employment – that is, at clerical or managerial level – for numbers running even into hundreds. Moreover a Government job was a job for life, and might even have a pension attached. The pay was not exciting except at the top of the service, which few clerks, entering at the bottom, could hope to reach, but the work was light – office hours, perhaps, ten to four – and a man of talent would not find it impossible to add to his income by writing.

In the early part of Queen Victoria's reign there was only one way into the Government service: patronage. Every appointment, from top to bottom, was in somebody's gift. In the civil departments the ultimate dispensers of patronage would be Ministers: in the Army and Navy, the Commander-in-Chief, the Lords of the Admiralty, and other officers and officials of high rank (a naval captain, for instance, had rights of patronage in the ship he commanded). Moreover in the Army there was the additional obstacle of purchase – that is, in addition to finding a patron, an intending officer in the infantry or cavalry (though not in the artillery, engineers or marines) usually had to buy his first commission, and after that every step in promotion.

Patronage was frequently and fruitily deplored (by those who did not benefit from it) in the eighteenth century and from the seventeen-eighties on fairly resolute attempts were made to reduce its scope, at least as far as total sinecures were concerned. Nevertheless it remained what it had been since time immemorial, and

23 *Left:* Rich mama is arranging to buy her son a commission while the veteran officer on the right is too poor to afford promotion.

24 *Right:* A modern recruiting poster for the army.

what it still is in a good many countries to-day: part of the texture of public life. Ministers relied on patronage to reward their supporters in Parliament, who expected to be listened to when they solicited places for friends, relations, and faithful voters. The voter, after all, was worthy of his hire – a principle not one whit affected by parliamentary reform – and friends and relations had to be provided for: one had a duty to them, had one not? 'I never yet served under a Secretary of State,' said a senior civil servant in 1854, approvingly, 'who did not, at least, appear to attach a very high interest indeed to the power of giving such places to his dependents and his friends.'

Patronage was part of politics. The middle classes were not political animals, and patronage was not in their hands. It lay in the grip of the traditional governing classes, which made honest middle-class hearts burn with the injustice of it all. 'The aristocracy of this country,' said Cobden in 1845, 'have the army, the navy, the colonies, and a large amount of expenditure, at their disposal.' The system was wrong. It must be changed, to allow true merit to triumph over aristocratic favouritism.

The patronage system lay wide open to attack because of the sheer inefficiency, in almost all departments, civil and military, of the Government service. The European revolutions of 1848 shook the complacency of official minds, and a five-year investigation of the work of public offices was put in hand, under a rising politician – Sir Stafford Northcote (1818–1887) – and the permanent head of the Treasury, Sir Charles Trevelyan (1807–1886). They had barely completed their report when the administrative scandals of the Crimean War, reported by W. H. Russell as the scandals of war had never been reported before, roused the middle classes to the same kind of action that had produced the repeal of the Corn Laws about ten years before.

The Administrative Reform Association was founded at a monster meeting in Drury Lane Theatre in June 1855. The Chairman could hardly have been a more representative middle-class figure. He was Samuel Morley (1809–1886), a non-conformist stocking-maker from Nottingham. 'He desired,' he is reported to have said, 'to see the offices of State thrown open to public competition, believing that every man possessed of talent was responsible for its employment for the benefit of his fellow-men.' At a great meeting in Birmingham, always a middle-class power-house, another representative figure – George Dawson, a surgeon – echoed Morley's demand: 'Now we demand that the whole system of England should be altered (Cheers). Not the Army only, not the Navy only, but all the Government affairs, all the Government offices; that all appointments shall be open to approved ability, tried by examination (Renewed Cheering).'

Northcote and Trevelyan had already earned the cheers of George Dawson's audience. Their *Report on the Organization of the Permanent Civil Service*, 1854, recommended, broadly speaking, that appointments in the home civil service should be made, as they already were in the Indian Civil Service, on the results of competitive examinations. No doubt the clamour made by Samuel Morley and his friends helped to get these recommendations hurried through. In 1855 the Civil Service Commission set to work, and over the following 110 years it moulded the service into the pattern which lasted until after the publication of the Fulton Report of 1965.

The assertion of the principle of competitive entry to the Government service took fifteen or twenty years to become fully effective, but by about 1875 the old official world of patronage, purchase (abolished in 1871), nepotism and interest had been turned upside down. Family influence remained important in the Army, the Royal Navy and the Diplomatic Service, but even in these it was made sub-ordinate to competitive prowess, and in any case these particular aristocratic pre-serves were not especially attractive to the middle classes. They were much more interested in the home civil service and the ics, and in both it had been established, by the mid-seventies, that the sole passport to a career would be success in competi-tive exams, chiefly written, and that 'interest' would have no bearing on the mat-ter whatever. As a consequence the general level of ability in both services rose, or perhaps it would be more correct to say that the level of ability in the upper division (later the administrative grade) of the home service rose to a level already attained in the ICS, and the attractions of a civil service career, including the financial attraction, became much greater.

It was not much use establishing qualifying examinations for entry into the professions, or competitive examinations for entry into the public service, unless there were schools where boys (and even girls) could get the education the examiners would be testing. Moreover education was a powerful aid to social climbing. It was therefore important for middle-class advancement, both professional and social, that the right sort of schools should exist or, if they did not exist, that they should be created. The matter was the more urgent because in the first half of the nineteenth century there was no State system of education (as there was in Germany and France) and the old grammar schools, for reasons which we have not space to explore, were far in decay.

The middle classes distrusted the State and believed in self-help. They therefore set about founding the kind of schools they thought they needed for their young. The growth of the railway system helped, because that made boarding schools more practical, and boarding schools, having a wider area than their immediate neighbourhood to draw on, could be more ambitious establishments than day schools, as well as providing middle-class parents with a country-wide choice of schools rather than a local one. Above all, perhaps, boarding schools were held to be unrivalled for inculcating the much-prized virtue of 'manliness' (which, amongst other things, would preserve boys from the danger of taking too much interest – better still, any interest at all – in the other sex).

25 Highgate School, founded as a grammar school in 1565, which, like many other old grammar schools, fell into decay in the nineteenth century and was rescued by a forceful Victorian headmaster, Dr Dyne (1839–74).

26

The models for these schools were the nine 'great schools' or 'public schools' (Eton, Winchester, Westminster, Charterhouse, St Paul's, Merchant Taylors', Harrow, Rugby, Shrewsbury) which, founded originally as 'grammar schools' more or less like all the rest, had grown until their reputation attracted 'the public' at large, rather than merely in their own vicinity. The nine differed considerably amongst themselves, but between them they had certain characteristics which had come to be considered distinguishing marks of 'public schools'.

All except two (St Paul's and Merchant Taylors', both in London) were boarding schools organised in 'houses', which were very profitable – much more profitable than teaching – for the fortunate masters who ran them. The system had grown up accidentally, because the original grammar school buildings made little or no provision for boarders, but Victorian house masters made great play with the moral uplift to be gained from 'house spirit'. All the 'great schools' except one (Eton) had some variant of the monitorial system, and with it generally went 'fagging'. The origin of the one seems to have been an insufficiency of staff to keep the boys properly in order, so that the eldest, or biggest, boys were required to take the place of assistant masters, and of the other, the natural tendency of big boys to make small boys run errands for them. By Victorian times, as with the house system, these fortuitous and slightly discreditable origins had acquired a fine patina of tradition, and Headmasters held them up to veneration as admirable vehicles, instituted by inscrutable ancestral wisdom, for the training of character.

The education in these schools was overwhelmingly classical, for the very good reason that university education was classical, and if university graduates were employed as schoolmasters, the classics were what they would teach. Anything else would be extra, little regarded, and very expensive. The classics were most uninspiringly taught, and as a refuge from the dreariness of it all, no doubt, and also in order to curb the natural ferocity of adolescent boys, bored and inadequately supervised, the schools developed a passion for team games, once again held up as magnificent stiffeners of all kinds of moral fibre, though that passion did not reach its ultimate pitch of intensity until towards the end of the century, when enthusiasm for games was matched only by a deep contempt for anything in the nature of artistic or intellectual activity.

40   Finally, there was no question that the public schools were intended to produce

gentlemen, even from the sons of shopkeepers, if the shopkeepers could pay the fees. More, if the formidable clerical headmasters had their way they would turn out *Christian* gentlemen – Church of England, naturally – and the best scholars among them might become parsons. Apart from religion, however, the principal business of gentlemen was government, and for government, or at least leadership, all public schoolboys were trained, though not specifically, until quite late in Victoria's reign, for the government of subject races. The Empire was not well thought of by the early Victorians, and headmasters of that period were apt to regard colonial appointments, and even appointments in India, as consolations for the second, third, or fourth best.

Between Victoria's early years and the turn of the century a great many boarding schools were founded, more or less (some very much more, some very much less) on the public school pattern. They varied from august establishments like Clifton, Cheltenham and Marlborough to the harum-scarum Imperial Service College at Westward Ho, described by Kipling, possibly a little larger than life-size, in *Stalky & Co.*

Many of these schools, like those already mentioned, were new foundations. Others, like Oundle, Sedbergh and Sherborne, were ancient grammar schools rescued and rejuvenated. Many were founded to serve a particular interest, religious or secular. There were schools for Roman Catholics, schools for Nonconformists, schools for the sons of doctors, or missionaries, of parsons, even of commercial travellers. All, broadly speaking, had the newly prosperous middle

27 From *Punch*, 1871:
'*Fond Father:* I see ye've put my son intil Graumer an' Jography. Noo, as I neither mean him tae be a minister or a sea-captain, it's o' nae use. Gie him a plain bizness eddication.'

classes in mind, and as a consequence they were obliged to cater for the world which the middle classes were creating: the world of business, of professional qualifications, of competitive examinations for the public service.

For this world the classical education of the 'great schools' was no longer enough, although it was long considered the highest form of education for a gentleman and/or a scholar. Rather reluctantly, for the most part, the new schools developed a 'modern side', covering mathematics, modern languages, English history and other subjects outside the classical syllabus – even, in some schools, running as far as science and engineering. The modern side was regarded by schoolmasters of the traditional kind (and schoolmasters are great traditionalists) as a poor substitute for a proper liberal education, and all the brightest boys, unless they or their parents were exceptionally strong-minded, continued to go up the classical side. Anything else was regarded, except by a few lonely eccentrics, as a necessary but unwelcome concession to the demands of nineteenth century materialism.

The more successful of these Victorian 'proprietary schools', as they were at first called, soon became known, like the nine 'great schools', as 'public schools', and it is under that title that the group as a whole has survived to the present day. Public schools are the most distinctively English contribution to secondary education. There has never been anything like them, except conscious imitations, elsewhere, and their influence has been enormous, though only a very small number of boys – probably less than 10 per cent of the relevant age group at any one time, have actually been to one. They have been taken as models for institutions as different as expensive boarding schools for girls, the secondary schools of the State system, when it came to be set up, and Borstals. They have always claimed, as their main educational virtue, the training of 'character'.

What kind of character?

28 A factory inspector of 1857 addressing mill girls on the virtue of thrift. 'Sixpence a day would, in seven years, produce £60 10s [£60.50] with which a man might build himself a house of his own.'

The public school man should be scornful of comfort and soft living and of all sensuous pleasure except life in the open air in hard physical conditions. He should expect to exercise leadership and he should accept responsibility for the welfare of those under him. He should be loyal and patriotic, though no doubt somewhat insensitive. In his relations with women he should be polite rather than passionate. Indeed by the public school code, as it developed late in the century, passion of any sort, except team spirit, is suspect, and it is from this extreme distrust, perhaps fear, of the emotions that the tradition of the English 'stiff upper lip' derives.

This is not the character of an eighteenth century Englishman of any class in society. It is the kind of character which might be expected from a blend of upper-class notions of honour, authority and responsibility with the Puritanism of the middle classes, the general tone of the mixture being set by the Puritanical element in it. In other words it is what might be expected of a middle-class take-over bid for the national character, and it must be admitted that so far as stock notions of English character are concerned, especially among foreigners, the bid has been a successful one.

By about 1875 middle-class influence on English society and institutions stood at high-water mark. Free Trade and *laissez-faire* economic policies had followed from their political victories in the thirties and forties. The professions had been reformed, expanded and improved. The upper-class grip on appointments in the public service had been destroyed, greatly to the national advantage. The public-school system, with several centuries of instant tradition, had been created. On all sides ancient institutions, picked up, dusted off, their works removed and totally new machinery inserted, were ticking away merrily in the service of the new masters. Poor-law reform, municipal reform, public health, fallen women, the drink problem, the alkali nuisance, the mission field, all these and many more bore witness to middle-class energy and drive. The middle class stood masters of the national field.

FURTHER READING

Muriel Jaeger, *Before Victoria*, changing standards and behaviour 1787–1837, Penguin edition.

David Newsome, *Godliness and Good Learning*, 1961.

Vivian Ogilvie, *The English Public School*, 1957.

W. J. Reader, *Professional Men*, the rise of the professional classes in nineteenth-century England, 1966.

Report on the Organization of the Permanent Civil Service, 1854 (the Northcote-Trevelyan Report).

4 Before the Bombardment

> That man, you may rely,
> Will be wealthy by and by
> If he'll only put his shoulder to the wheel.
>
> Victorian song.

In Heaven there is an eternal tea-party on the Rectory lawn. The Rector, full-bearded, benignly authoritarian (Jehovah has taken Anglican orders) moves among his guests, who include the Squire, the Doctor, and the man who is 'something in the City', yet a perfect gentleman whose son has gone to Marlborough. Well-trained servants, including one dusky Christian convert, hand round and wash up. Beneath the ancient elms *The Times* is read (if you don't believe *The Times* circulates in Heaven, look at the In Memoriam notices). Beyond the garden gate the June sun shines on thatched rustic wisdom and gnarled content. The bounds of Heaven are patrolled by angels with flaming swords, but somehow they all have the look of the sailor on the *Players'* packet. God is an Englishman, and Time has finally stopped about four in the afternoon, somewhere between 1870 and 1914.

That, at any rate, is rather how matters have seemed, ever since 1914, to people who identify themselves with the prosperous classes of late Victorian England – which can include those who identify with the servants as well as those who identify with the masters. Those who identify themselves with neither naturally have a different idea of Heaven, and it may be nearer to the present day. Even for the

29 This house was designed for a country clergyman living near Montacute in Somerset, who was 'anxious to have a residence in the old decorated style of wooden architecture, certainly the most picturesque of all the styles our forefathers have left us'. It included servants' rooms and wine and beer cellars.

30 John Player's 'sailor' trade mark.

majority of middle-class people, late Victorian life was less delightful than mythology suggests. The myth perpetuates, however, a memory of middle-class ascendancy which was real enough. Let us examine the reality behind the myth.

By the last quarter of the nineteenth century the middle classes had come a long way from the eighteenth century country towns where first we met them, frugal, busy, obscure. A new industrial world had been created, largely by their own energy, which gave much greater scope for their talents. Some middle-class men had made or were making large fortunes from activities as diverse as soda ash (John Brunner and Ludwig Mond), heavy guns and the ships to carry them (W. G. Armstrong), household soap (W. H. Lever), and black crepe for the panoply of Victorian grief (Samuel Courtauld and his relations).

Below this level and perhaps even more important, because more widespread, there was the moderate prosperity of middle-class families, all over the country, in small and smallish businesses and in the ever-widening range of professional, semi-professional and would-be professional occupations which the new economic life of the country needed and could support. 'Every department of skilled industry,' said a social commentator (W. H. S. Escott) of the late seventies, '. . . has annexed to it, so to speak, a considerable specialist business of its own. The development of commerce has been the opportunity for creating a host of occupations. . . . Art has proved scarcely less productive. . . . There is not only more work for painters of creative genius than ever, but for a class of artists who never existed before – decorators and designers of all kinds and in all materials. In literature the same movement has, or will have soon, been experienced, and journalism has certainly acquired a true professional status.'

These easier circumstances, and a sense of established position, made for an easier, less austere way of life. The late Victorian middle classes were less ferociously puritanical than their fathers and grandfathers, and their religious practice showed it. Regular church-going was required for respectability, but as families moved up the social scale they were inclined also to move into the parish church, away from Nonconformity.

Nonconformity, nevertheless, was still strong among the middle classes, as all Victorian politicians knew. 'Ours is not the Church of the poor,' said a Congregationalist minister of the nineties, and much the same might have been said of the main body of Methodists. The enormous complexes of church buildings, with Sunday schools and halls, often on several storeys, alongside the church itself, which well-to-do Nonconformists put up in well-to-do districts, still survive, usually somewhat bedraggled, to prove the point.

Nonconformity in these surroundings was less rigorous than in the early part of the century. A London Congregational church in a middle-class district would have a busy social life, and a good deal of the activity might have little to do with religion – a Literary Society, perhaps, or a Mutual Improvement Society, a tennis club or a camera club. This does not sound unbearably exacting, and indeed Charles Booth, the sociologist who reported it, evidently considered the religious life of the Congregationalists tranquil to the point of smugness. Their influence, he thought, 'is more social than religious, but it is good and wholesome, and being without exaltation is free from the dangers of reaction'.

The generally rather more relaxed attitude – the degree of relaxation must not be exaggerated – spread to habits of work. In Government offices, in the old unregenerate days of patronage, hours had been short, and even in the brisk air of competitive entry they grew no longer. In private business clerks, until well after mid-century, had been required to be in the office for twelve hours, and that gradually shortened. By 1906 the offices of the Nobel-Dynamite Trust in London opened at 9.30 am and closed at 5 pm, with an ample interval for lunch, and overtime rates were paid for work done after 5 pm. In that office the seniors used occasionally to shoo their juniors away while they settled down to cards, but that may not have been typical of Edwardian business.

Late Victorian business men at the top – partners, managers, directors – have often been accused, in their own day and since, of taking life altogether too easily and showing deplorable lack of enterprise while German and American competitors raced past them. There is a degree of truth in the charge, but it is difficult to make it stick generally. For every idler or stick-in-the-mud who is quoted it is fairly easy to anti-quote an energetic innovator, though not necessarily in the same trade. Contemporary records of three important late Victorian firms – Brunner, Mond (a forerunner of ICI) in chemicals, Lever Bros in soap, G. & J. Weir in engineering – suggest hard work and untiring travel by the founders and their immediate successors. Some of them, once the business was fairly going, withdrew to other pursuits, especially politics, but that was a normal development of a suc-

46

31 William Hesketh Lever, 1st Viscount Leverhulme (1851–1925). He was a Bolton grocer's son who made a fortune out of soap and built up a huge grocery business, which today belongs to Unilever, founded 1929 by a merger between Lever Brothers Ltd. and two Dutch margarine firms.

32 From *Punch*, 1909:
'*Eminent Artist:* I'm glad to see, Sir Multimill, that you have a little work of mine in your corridor.
Bloated Plutocrat: Oh . . . 'Ave I?'

cessful man's career which could be paralleled in the careers of foreign competitors.

Whether or not the owners of businesses conducted their affairs lackadaisically while they were nominally in charge, there was a subtler temptation which beset them, especially in the second or third generation, and they have equally been berated for it. This was the temptation to desert business altogether for snobbish reasons, and especially to become country gentlemen, as generations of successful English businessmen, all the way back to the Middle Ages, had done before them. The newly rich squire was a target for satire in his own generation and has been sniped at since, but if he applied his capital shrewdly he could rescue a derelict estate and in the business he had left there would be no lack of professional managers eager to replace him. They might be better businessmen, too.

There can never have been many families rich enough to set up as large landed proprietors and those who did may have attracted undue attention. What was probably more important was the strong disinclination, among well-to-do young men of high ability, to follow their fathers in the traditional occupation of the middle classes – business. The nation's welfare depended on business, and it needed high ability at least as much as the Government service, the professions, scholarship, journalism and the arts, but it did not get its fair share. Indeed it got practically no share at all. In the last twenty or thirty years before 1914, with the growth in size of firms, there was an increasing need for professional managers, but it was almost unheard-of for a young man with a good degree to think of taking his talents into the market-place, though in Germany and America it was already fairly common.

Why the English reluctance?

'Business' or 'trade' had never been considered an occupation fit for gentlemen, and in the state of commercial morality prevailing in the early nineteenth century, especially at the lower end, there was some justification for this disdain, though gentlemen had often overcome it when their family fortunes needed restoring, either by going into trade themselves or by marrying into it. Anti-commercial prejudice, nevertheless, was firmly built into the old educational system – the nine 'great schools' and the universities of Oxford and Cambridge – and when the new public schools were founded they took it over. Through their immense influence a gentleman's education came to be associated, in the rising middle-class mind, with predominantly classical training, especially for the brightest boys, with neglect of science ('stinks'), and with a contempt for commercial pursuits.

Victorian headmasters could not afford to be so other-worldly as to ignore altogether the demand of middle-class parents that their sons, for the most part, should be trained to earn a living, repugnant though that might be to their own ideas of the true purpose of education, 'which is,' wrote Edward Thring of Uppingham, 'mental and bodily training in the best way, apart from immediate gain'. They preferred, however, and in this they had the support of parents, to direct their pupils' ambitions towards occupations intellectually and socially more distinguished than 'trade'.

The result was a split in the middle classes between the professional class and the rest. A doctor might have a grocer, perhaps much wealthier than himself, as a patient, but he would not meet him socially, nor would the children of the two families play together. Matthew Arnold, as early as 1866, noticed and deplored the split. He linked it with the 'cast of ideas' propagated by 'half a dozen famous schools, Oxford or Cambridge' which 'judged from its good side, is characterized by a high spirit, by dignity, by a just sense of the greatness of great affairs – all of them governing qualities', but 'judged from its bad side, . . . is characterized by its indisposition and incapacity for science, for systematic knowledge.' In consequence, he said, the professions 'are . . . in England separate, to a degree unknown on the Continent, from the commercial and industrial class with which in social standing they are naturally on a level. So we have amongst us the spectacle of a middle class cut in two in a way unexampled anywhere else; of a professional class brought up . . . with fine and governing qualities, but without the idea of

33 Whitley's of Bayswater, one of the first 'department stores' (anything from an elephant to a second-hand coffin) in the 1880s.

science; while that immense business class . . . on which the future so much depends . . . is in England . . . cut off from the aristocracy, and the professions, and without governing qualities.'

In the secure world of the affluent late Victorian middle classes it was easy to ignore or belittle the damaging effects of this split and of mounting foreign competition, especially from Germany. As Matthew Arnold hinted, there was a connection between the two, but both could be pushed to one side of the mind by a well-to-do Englishman who knew that the British did more foreign trade than anyone else;

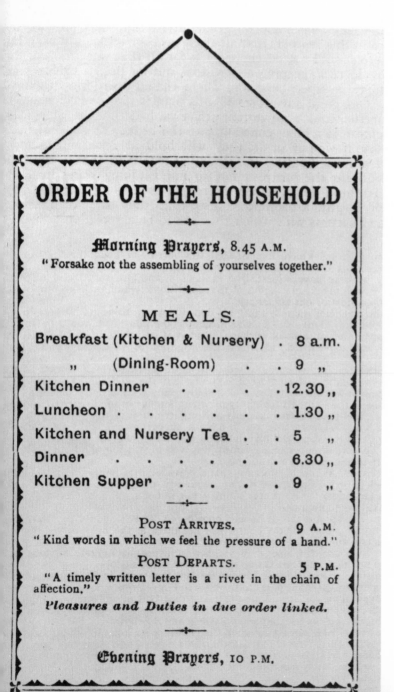

ORDER OF THE HOUSEHOLD

Morning Prayers, 8.45 A.M.
"Forsake not the assembling of yourselves together."

MEALS.

Breakfast (Kitchen & Nursery)	8 a.m.
„ (Dining-Room)	9 „
Kitchen Dinner	12.30 „
Luncheon	1.30 „
Kitchen and Nursery Tea	5 „
Dinner	6.30 „
Kitchen Supper	9 „

POST ARRIVES. 9 A.M.
" Kind words in which we feel the pressure of a hand."
POST DEPARTS. 5 P.M.
"A timely written letter is a rivet in the chain of affection."
Pleasures and Duties in due order linked.

Evening Prayers, 10 P.M.

34 From Mrs. Beeton's *Household Management,* 1895 edition.

who could travel over something like a quarter of the earth's surface in perfect safety, under the protection of British power; and who was persuaded that the mass of the population, though not nearly so well off as he was, was nevertheless much better off than ever before. 'The poor,' said the President of the Royal Statistical Society in 1884, 'have . . . had almost all the benefit of the great material advance of the last fifty years.' Statistics, no doubt, can be made to prove anything.

The middle class take-over bid had succeeded so well that long before the end of the nineteenth century the upper middle class, in their own estimation, were indistinguishable from the representatives of the old governing class, whom they had tamed without overthrowing. They went to the same schools and the same universities. Their sons took commissions in the army, which under the purchase system had been quite beyond the middle-class ken. They provided civil servants at home, in the colonies and in India. They provided Joseph Chamberlain, the Birmingham screw manufacturer who at one time looked rather like a future Conservative Prime Minister. They provided a Liberal Prime Minister, Asquith, and his wife, the daughter of a Glasgow business man, Sir Charles Tennant, who from his ample supply also provided a wife for Lord Ribblesdale, the Master of Queen Victoria's Buckhounds, and higher than that in the social scale it was scarcely possible to go.

In one respect the new upper class differed profoundly from the old. They were not countrymen, although that was what they did their best to turn into. Their way of making a living, however, kept them tied to towns, as the middle class always has been tied, and unless they could afford to leave business altogether they were obliged to make that compromise between town and country life which is suburbia. As the suburban railways pushed further and further outwards from London, Manchester, Birmingham, Glasgow, so the 'commodious residences' sprang up around the stations on the line – solid, detached houses in every form of architecture from plainest of the plain to wildest Venetian or Byzantine, with carriage drive, ample accommodation, billiard room and wine cellar. One such house in Wimbledon, bought about 1908 by a tin-box maker from Worcester, had two and a half acres of garden, coach houses, and a staff of nine indoors and out. Houses of this kind, though still in good order, are nowadays being rapidly swept away, because the grounds can be developed to carry a dozen or more houses instead of one: a very profitable proposition.

The suburbs bred sports clubs. To the old-fashioned gentry 'sport' meant hunting, shooting, fishing, horse racing, but the hunt in full cry cannot gallop down Putney High Street and the boys in the new public schools were brought up to ball games, and these were the games of the suburbs. Clubs were formed for football of both sorts (the rules settled down in the sixties and seventies), cricket, golf. Lawn tennis came in during the seventies (a version was patented by Major W. C. Wingfield [1833–1912] in 1873 under the name *Sphairistike*) and it was played on the lawns of private houses, as croquet was also, by both men and women.

35 A house designed about 1900 to be built for £2,350, with four bedrooms on the first floor, four more in the attic. A house appropriate to one's social standing, it was generally assumed, could be bought for the value of one year's income.

From the sixties onward another game became popular – soldiers, in the form of the Volunteers, who blossomed into Territorials in 1907. At the War Office they regarded the amateurs with a good deal of scepticism, but the middle classes took them very seriously. 'Captain' or 'Major' – better still, 'Colonel' – looked very well in front of one's name at the head of the firm's notepaper, especially if it had VD (Volunteer Decoration) after it as well.

Somewhat freer social conventions and greater physical safety in towns adequately policed, at any rate in respectable districts, made for easier and less formal relations between men and women. They played tennis together, they rode bicycles together, they roller-skated. More: fashionable married women might live lives of their own 'in which the husband only figures as an occasional visitor'. This was in the late seventies. Escott, who reported it, found female emancipation heady stuff: 'The liberty is still a little new, and it may be that the deep draughts of it which are taken are a little too powerful for our as yet unseasoned social system.'

Girls – some girls – were being educated, too, in subjects which had formerly been considered fit only for men. Alongside the new public schools, schools were

36 'Women's Lib.' 1869: fishing, croquet (introduced into England in the 1850s), and riding (side-saddle, of course).

founded which were designed to give girls a full academic course instead of the smattering of general knowledge and 'accomplishments' which were all that had previously been administered to them. By 1853 three of these schools – Queen's College, Harley Street, the North London Collegiate School and Cheltenham Ladies' College – were in existence, and in the sixties the assault on Oxford and Cambridge began.

This was still unorthodox and rather improper. It was even worse for a woman of good social standing to earn her own living unless she had to, and if she had to that in itself was a disgrace. Nevertheless from the late fifties onward determined ladies were butting their way into the medical profession against outraged, frightened and ludicrous male opposition. *Punch*, that faithful mirror of the middle-class mind, is full of anti-woman jokes in the sixties and seventies, showing how deeply the men feared and resented the female onslaught.

The life of the affluent suburbs, with troops of servants, children at expensive boarding schools, showy entertaining and long, elaborate holidays at home and

37 Girton College was established outside Cambridge in 1869; Newnham in 1871; the first two women's colleges at Oxford (Somerville and Lady Margaret Hall) in 1879. This drawing of 1869 *The Sisters' University* seems to satirize the beer-drinking and duelling of the German universities.

38 'Supper table with floral decorations arranged for sixteen persons', from Mrs. Beeton's *Household Management*, 1895 edition.

abroad, was imitated, more and more distantly, right down the middle-class scale to families keeping up appearances in terrace houses on £150 a year or so. Even at this level, according to the 1895 edition of Mrs Beaton's *Household Management*, there might be a 'general servant, or girl for rough work', and the 'scale of servants suited to various incomes' – not including nurse-maids – was:

About £1,000 a year – Cook, upper and under housemaid, man servant.
About £750 a year – Cook, housemaid, and man servant.
About £500 a year – Cook, housemaid, and foot-boy.
About £300 a year – Cook and housemaid.
About £200 or £150 a year – General servant, or girl for rough work.

The lower middle classes, like the upper, were divided amongst themselves, but along rather different lines. The question of professional status hardly arose, except among the teachers, who were perpetually trying to convince everyone else that they had achieved it. The main division lay between those who ran their own businesses and those who worked for some one else, chiefly as clerks.

Small business men – shopkeepers, builders and others in the towns; farmers in the countryside – were regarded with contempt by their social superiors, especially professional men, and with suspicion by the rest of the community. They were supposed to embody the worst middle-class attributes – narrow-mindedness corrupted by hypocrisy, and devotion to the profit motive at its meanest. They had the reputation of being among the harshest of employers – Victorian shop assistants' hours have become legendary, and farm labourers were notoriously underpaid and bullied – and as ratepapers it was evident to all that they grudged more than the barest minimum for municipal services.

This was not how they saw themselves, of course. They considered themselves God-fearing, law-abiding, hard-working and, above all, self-supporting, as everyone ought to be. Of course they were careful about their profits, for the alternative to profit was ruin. Of course they resented an extra penny on the rates, because that usually meant looking after people who should be looking after themselves. Wasn't it enough to provide employment, and shouldn't those who were employed be decently grateful for it? Didn't the more prosperous townsmen, in any case, from time to time bestow upon their fellow citizens public baths, public parks, town halls, drinking fountains and all manner of other amenities? Did they not take it upon themselves, in many towns, to reorganise the ancient grammar schools, so that those who did not aspire to 'public schools' could once again get decent education not far from their own doorstep? They did all these things, especially in the two Jubilee years, 1887 and 1897, and all over England their monuments proclaim the exuberance of late Victorian civic pride.

Besides the self-employed, the other main group in the lower middle classes consisted of people in minor salaried jobs, and of these, in the years before 1914, the most conspicuous were those recorded by the Census authorities as 'commercial

39 and **40**   Kitchen and drawing room of a brewery manager's house in a country town (Chipping Norton), probably about 1910.

clerks': that is, clerks in private business, not Government offices. Their numbers were rising much faster than the numbers in most other middle class occupations. There were under 50,000 commercial clerks in 1841. In 1881 there were over 180,000, and 477,000 in 1911.

This rise in numbers was important for three reasons. First, it showed that the old bugbear of the middle classes – lack of salaried employment – was becoming rather less oppressive. Secondly, here was a nursery of professional management for the larger industrial undertakings which were coming into being. Clerks could become accountants, sales managers, buyers, just as engineers could become works managers. Thirdly, 'commercial clerks' included typists, and 'type-writers', as they were at first called, were mainly women almost from the start. Along with telephone exchanges, typing pools greatly widened the opportunities of earning an independent living which were open to middle-class women. The typewriter has done more for women's liberation than it is usually given credit for, and much more than any other mechanical invention, except perhaps the bicycle.

At the top of the social scale, as we have seen, the upper middle classes of pre-1914 England merged almost imperceptibly into the traditional governing class, whose roots were in landed property. At the lower end, equally imperceptibly, the clerks and small independent tradesmen shaded away into what Charles Booth

41 'The brewer handing £522 10s [£522.50] to Alderman Beaumont for the Temperance Society'. From the brewer's point of view gin was the sinful drink, not beer. *British Workman*, 1859.

42 The official opening of Guilford Castle Grounds in 1888, with the Mayor, Aldermen, Councillors and other worthies.

in the nineties called 'the comfortable working class'. He said it was the largest section of the people, 'and is thus, more than any other, representative of "the way we live now"'. At what Booth called 'the summit of working class life' were 'foremen and highly paid artisans', earning 40s (£2) to 70s (£3·50) a week, with other members of the family bringing in money as well.

The artisans of late Victorian England ran their lives, broadly speaking, on middle-class principles of respectability, regularity, sobriety and hard work.

43 and **44** John Bull in fact (1910), and fiction (*Punch*, 1909).

They were religious, usually Nonconformist, and they distinguished themselves sharply from 'rough' and 'common' people lower in the social order. They were the backbone of the craft unions, and they were not pleased by the rise of unions among unskilled workers in the nineties.

The Reform Act passed by Lord Derby's Conservative government of 1867 gave the vote to men of this class, being the first approach to general democracy in English history, though 'democracy' remained a dirty word in the Establishment's dictionary of politics until well into the eighties, if not longer. In the forties, many voters of this class might have been revolutionary Chartists, but Chartism was dead by 1867. The day of socialism and class warfare had not yet come, and it would be many years before ideas of this sort would take widespread root among the 'respectable working class'.

Altogether, as the twentieth century began, the middle-class bid for total take-over of English society might have seemed, on a superficial view, very close to success. Unfortunately the self-confidence of the prosperous classes showed every sign of going addle and degenerating into smugness. It was perhaps appropriate that the chosen symbolic figure of the nation, John Bull, should be shown by cartoonists over-weight, middle-aged, irascible, dressed in clothes almost 100 years out of date. The permanence of things, however, even of middle-class smugness, was by no means so rock-solid as it seemed.

FURTHER READING

T. H. S. Escott, *England, its People, Polity and Pursuits*, 1879 (reprinted – 5th Edn – by Frank Cass, London).

M. Vivian Hughes, *A London Family 1870–1900*, 1951.

John Galsworthy, *The Forsyte Saga*.

George & Weedon Grossmith, *Diary of a Nobody*.

Mrs Beeton, *Household Management*, any edition before 1914.

Yesterday's Shopping, the Army & Navy Store's Catalogue 1907 reprinted by David & Charles, 1969.

Punch, bound volumes.

5 The Crisis of Conscience

No one ever lost money by taking a profit.

Trad. (Stock Exchange)

'Let a man go where he will, he is beset on every side with the exclusiveness of private property. The public has kept nothing.' These words were published in 1851. The protest of some belated Chartist? An unnoticed observation, perhaps, of the young Karl Marx (1818–1883)?

Neither. This is the middle-class conscience at work. The passage comes from *England as it is . . . in the middle of the nineteenth century*,* two volumes by William Johnston, a barrister of high Tory opinions. Like many Tories, including Disraeli, Johnston disliked what he saw of '*laissez-faire*', that central principle of middle-class ascendancy.

He went on to discuss 'the actual state of the poor throughout England', and concluded: '. . . their physical distress, their ignorance, and their vices are the true fruits of the system of "letting alone", in other words of leaving men to practise for their own advancement all arts save actual violence; of allowing every natural and every artificial superiority to enjoy and push its advantages to the utmost, and of suffering the weaker to pay the full penalty of their inferiority.'

It was possible to argue, and indeed many did, that the poor brought their own misfortunes upon themselves, chiefly through their 'unrestrained appetite for drink'. There was nothing wrong with the system that self-control would not cure, and only self-control could cure it: 'No reform of institutions, no extended power of voting, no improved form of government, no amount of scholastic instruction, can possibly elevate the character of a people who voluntarily abandon themselves to sensual indulgence. The pursuit of ignoble pleasure is the degradation of true happiness; it saps the morals, destroys the energies, and degrades the manliness and robustness of individuals as of nations.'

That is Samuel Smiles, writing in 1871, and no doubt he represented orthodox middle-class opinion much more accurately than Johnston. Nevertheless there was great uneasiness, and as early as the forties some of those who knew most about the problems of poverty, notably Southwood Smith, were beginning to doubt whether self-control was an all-sufficient answer. It was obvious that heavy drinking and slum housing, with its attendant evils of ignorance, disease and malnutrition, went together, but perhaps it was the bad housing that caused the heavy drinking, rather than the other way about?

* *England as it is, Political, Social and Industrial in the Middle of the Nineteenth Century.*

45 'Model houses for the Labouring Classes, exhibited by Prince Albert' at the Great Exhibition 1851. He 'has not disdained to give careful consideration to the condition of the hard-working artisan'. The houses were designed as blocks of four with three bedrooms each providing 'that separation . . . so essential to morality and decency'.

Certainly bad housing, as well as heavy drinking, was one of the main targets of middle-class reformers concerned with the social disasters of industrialisation. Their method of improving it, typically, was not by demanding state intervention but by private effort. Prince Albert, indefatigable patron of worthy causes, designed a pair of 'model cottages' for the Great Exhibition of 1851, and by the seventies large blocks of flats – 'model dwellings' – were becoming part of the London scene, especially those built by the Peabody Trust, founded in 1862 by George Peabody (1795–1869), an American merchant settled in London (there is a statue near the Bank of England).

The spirit of these enterprises was brisk, energetic, orderly. Nothing was to be given away for nothing, and the rents were calculated to show sufficient profit for upkeep. Much of the driving force came from Miss Octavia Hill (1838–1912), a redoubtable lady, influenced as a girl by the Christian Socialists and John Ruskin. She spoke rather bleakly of 'a life of law . . . not developing any great individuality, but consistent with happy home-life, and it promises to be the life of the respectable London working-man.' She supported the Charity Organisation Society, which existed to see that the large sums given to charity did not go to the 'undeserving', and was not very popular with the poor in consequence. Benevolent, certainly, but authoritarian in the manner of her day, Octavia Hill and others like her were figures of respect rather than affection.

Of a rather similar turn of mind were those Victorian employers, and they were numerous, who attended to the welfare of their employees. 'There could be no worse friend to Labour,' said W. H. Lever in 1909, 'than the benevolent, philanthropic employer who carries on his business in a loose, lax manner, showing "kindness" to his employees; because . . . sooner or later he will be compelled to close.' The outlook of employers like Lever – the good Victorian employers – was paternalistic. Speaking of a profit-sharing scheme, Lever himself said: '£8 . . . will not do you much good if you send it down your throats in the form of bottles of whisky, bags of sweets, or fat geese for Christmas. On the other hand, if you leave this money with me, I shall use it to provide for you everything which makes life pleasant – viz. nice houses, comfortable homes, and healthy recreation. Besides, I am disposed to allow profit sharing under no other than that form.'

Paternalism, in late Victorian England, had not acquired the undesirable associations which have clustered round it since, and any notion of 'participation' or workers' control might have astonished the workers as much as it would certainly have outraged the employers. The Victorian employer, like the Victorian parent, 'knew best,' and contemporary opinion did not expect children or employees to question their elders' and/or betters' wisdom, particularly when it was directed to their own good. Their place was to take what they were given and be grateful.

On the whole, they probably were. There was no legal compulsion on an employer in Victorian England to take care of his men, but many did, and got some thanks for it. As late as 1923, when benevolence of the old paternalistic kind was becoming suspect, members of the Amalgamated Engineering Union and the Boiler Makers' Union presented an illuminated address to the Directors of Brunner, Mond in which they said:

We . . . desire to place on record our appreciation of the manner in which you have always striven to improve the Education of those in your employ, and also of the example you set to the Industrial World by your adoption of the Eight Hour Day and Holiday System.

Many of the more enlightened Victorian employers' welfare schemes – medical services, sick benefits, holidays-with-pay, canteens, sports clubs – have become so commonplace as to seem unremarkable to-day, or else they have been submerged in the much greater flood of welfare from the State. Bricks and mortar, however, still remain, including houses, churches, schools, mechanics' institutes and, occasionally, hospitals. The Great Western Railway built New Swindon, in the general style of the nearby Cotswold villages, in the forties. Sir Titus Salt began building Saltaire, flamboyantly Italianate (in the West Riding!), in the fifties. About thirty years later came the beginning of Cadburys' Bournville and of Lever's Port Sunlight, which Lever used irritably to insist was *not* an advertisement for Sunlight Soap. They are all monuments which still do credit to their founders.

46 Port Sunlight, Cheshire, founded by William Lever, 1888, for the workers in his soap factory. 'I shall . . . provide for you everything which makes life pleasant' – Lever, 1903. 'No man of an independent turn of mind can breathe for long the atmosphere of Port Sunlight' – Secretary of Bolton Branch of Engineers' Union, 1919.

Lever and other like-minded employers were far from intending any fundamental criticism of the industrial system. It had given them wealth and power, which naturally coloured their view of it, but equally they could see what it had done for the well-being of the nation as a whole, and they were not disposed to think that any other system could do better. Employers of this type were not, in general, inclined to conservatism in politics – rather, indeed, to radicalism, but radicalism in a nineteenth century sense, firmly wedded to private capitalism and suspicious of the State. Sir John Brunner (1842–1919), called by his biographer a 'radical plutocrat', thought socialism 'impossible of attainment by the hands of men; it requires angels', and perhaps he has not yet been proved wrong.

The industrial system came under attack almost from the start. The most famous partnership in the revolutionary business – the firm of Marx & Engels, as *bourgeois* a pair in their origins as it would be possible to find – was set up in the eighteen-forties, and in 1848 their *Communist Manifesto* set out the doctrine of class warfare. Greatly elaborated, it was to become the central theory of left-wing politics, of the Russian Revolution, and of communist states when they came to be set up. The *bourgeoisie* – the middle classes – were presented unequivocally as the enemies of the mass of working-class people and their overthrow, along with the whole system of thought, religion, morals and general culture associated with them – was alleged to be necessary, and was confidently predicted, before the only just society – communism – could be established.

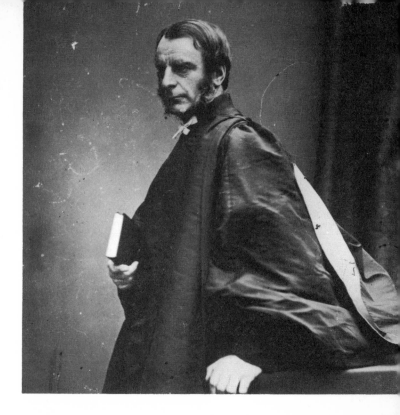

47 Canon Charles Kingsley (1819–1875), novelist, pamphleteer, Christian Socialist, though he 'never adopted the socialist creed in a sense which could now shock the most conservative'.

Marx and Engels, both German, worked in England and their criticism of capitalist society was largely based on English experience, since in their day industrial capitalism in England, having had a long start, had developed much further than anywhere else. The English middle classes themselves, however, scarcely needed prompting to observe the dark side of industrialisation. Their collective conscience rapidly turned its strong self-critical cutting edge on the system which the middle classes had very largely created. To go no further back than the middle of the century, attacks from various directions were delivered by Carlyle, Ruskin, Charles Dickens, Mrs Gaskell and the group who called themselves 'Christian Socialists' (Charles Kingsley, Thomas Hughes, F. D. Maurice), though they were not socialists in the Marxist sense. William Morris and Matthew Arnold, deeply disturbed by the ugliness of it all, added their voices in the sixties and later. '*Philistine*,' wrote Matthew Arnold in *Culture and Anarchy*, 'gives the notion of something particularly stiff-necked and perverse in the resistance to light and its children, and therein it specially suits our middle class.' Even Cobden, in a moment of exasperation, once referred to 'leather-headed bipeds' – and he meant the English middle classes.

In the midst of all this indignation was the spectacle of poverty, the central social problem of Victorian England. Poverty was exhaustively investigated, publicly and privately, throughout the century. The state of large towns was examined, at the instance of Edwin Chadwick (1800–1890), in the forties, and the housing of the working classes in the eighties. If anything, the disgustingness revealed at the later enquiry was worse than at the earlier. Sanitation, white slavery, child labour, venereal disease, farm labourers' wages, depression in trade

48 A cartoon from the *Voice of Labour*, 1907, entitled 'Man of the Hour':

'*One of the Smart Set* (doing London): I suppose we shall have to go and hear Shaw, Bertie. I understand that he is very amusing.

Bertie: Oh yes, awfully, awfully! It is considered quite the thing now for our people to go and listen to him. He is so awfully, bally, beastly absurd, don't you know.'

and industry – all these and much more were brought under official enquiry, which left very few aspects of the life of the poor unexamined.

Alongside the parliamentary enquiries, sociology was developing. Henry Mayhew (1812–1887), a journalist, investigated the lower depths of London life in the fifties. Charles Booth (1840–1916), a wealthy shipowner, organised a team of investigators to carry out a far more elaborate enquiry, reported in nine volumes, in the nineties. Public schools and colleges of Oxford and Cambridge, following an example set by Thring of Uppingham, set up 'missions' in the East End of London where well-to-do young men found out what life was like for the large minority of the population – Booth put it at 30 per cent – who lived in poverty.

During the eighties, left-wing politics on the modern pattern – with a Marxist foundation – began to emerge. H. M. Hyndman (1842–1921), a journalist, founded the Social Democratic Federation in 1881, and for a while attracted William Morris into it. In 1884 the Fabian Society, a pressure-group of intellectuals, aiming at a gradual socialist takeover, came into existence. During the bad trade of 1885–1886 Hyndman's SDF organised demonstrations among the unemployed, and after a riot in and near Trafalgar Square on 7th February 1886 Hyndman, with others, was arrested.

During the eighties the British political scene was enriched and sometimes enlivened by the emergence of what was to become a familiar twentieth century figure: the middle-class, left-wing intellectual. Among the earliest were G. B. Shaw (1856–1950) the (Anglo-)Irishman; Sidney Webb (1859–1947) and his formidable wife Beatrice (1858–1943) (who narrowly missed becoming Mrs Joseph Chamberlain instead); and H. G. Wells (1866–1946), from a lower social drawer ('son of unsuccessful tradesman,' says the Dictionary of National Biography, with a professional-class sniff). With wit, pugnacity and quarrelsome energy they threw themselves into British public life at the national and local level, working, writing, intriguing indefatigably for the advancement of socialist ends. The possibilities of applying left-wing thought to neglected academic subjects, such as

49 The Fabian Society were an intellectual group with socialist sympathies.

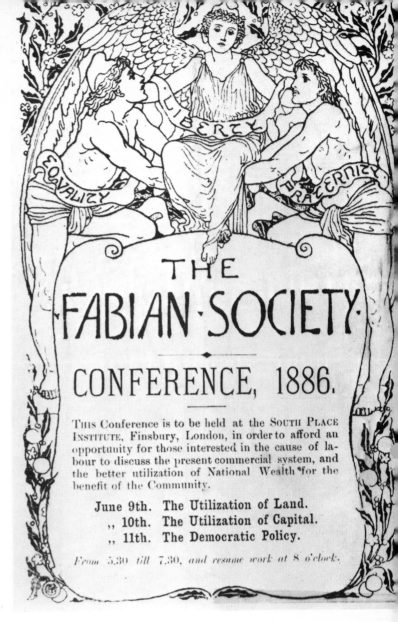

economic history, began to be explored. In 1895, with a mighty shove from the Webbs, the London School of Economics and Political Science, that great power-house of left-wing thought, was founded.

The position of the left-wing intellectuals of the middle class has always been fundamentally uneasy. Well-to-do, well-connected, well-educated, as many of them were and have continued to be, they have had little in common with the working man, who has always known it. Nevertheless conscience, that highly-developed moral muscle of the middle-class mind, has propelled them into the Labour Party, a party dedicated to the destruction of their own class, the members of which naturally respond with suspicion or outright hostility. The middle-class intellectual has often been further to the left than the natural representatives of labour from the trade unions, and the alliance between the two wings of the

50 Sidney Webb, Lord Passfield (1859–1947) and his wife Beatrice (1858–1943). Joint authors of *The History of Trade Unionism* (1894), *Industrial Democracy* (1897), *English Local Government* (1906–29), and much else. They expected social progress to come from the influence of an *élite*.

Labour Movement has never been an easy one: the more so since many of the political leaders, including one of the most outstandingly successful Prime Ministers of any party, Clement Attlee, have come from the middle classes. The Labour Party, as it has grown up over the last fifty years, no doubt represents working-class interests, but it has been very much a middle-class creation.

Intellectuals of the left often represent a tradition of plain living and high thinking, combined with sympathetic regard for the unfortunate, which was one of the finest elements in late Victorian middle-class life – Puritanism with some of the cragginess worn down. It is no accident that their background was often a professional-class household, perhaps clerical, where there was a stronger regard for public duty and for integrity than for immediate gain. But although the emergence of this group was in a well-established middle-class tradition, it represented a debilitating crisis of conscience in the middle-class mind. Doubt began to undermine self-confidence, and the process, gradual at first and little regarded, began to accelerate rapidly under the shock of the Great War.

FURTHER READING

Matthew Arnold, *Culture and Anarchy*, 1889.

Karl Marx, *Economy, Class and Social Revolution* (selected writings, ed. Z. A. Jordan), 1971.

Bernard Shaw, *The Bodley Head Bernard Shaw*, 1970.

Beatrice Webb, *My Apprenticeship*, 1926.

6 On the Defensive

God send you fortune, yet be sure,
    Among the lights that gleam and pass,
You'll live to follow none more pure
    Than that which gleams on yonder brass:
Qui procul hinc, the legend's writ, –
    The frontier-grave is far away –
Qui ante diem periit:
    Sed miles, sed pro patria.
                Sir Henry Newbolt (1862–1938) *Clifton Chapel*, 1898.*

The old Lie: *Dulce et decorum est pro patria mori.**
            Wilfred Owen (1893–1918) *Dulce et Decorum est*, 1918.

At the end of the Great War the middle classes, in common with the rest of the nation, found themselves surveying the badly shaken structure of Victorian England. The damage was not physical. All about them stood the Victorian cities, the Victorian suburbs, the Victorian railways, the Victorian factories – the entire material framework of the industrial society which had come rapidly into existence, under middle-class leadership, during the nineteenth century.

The damage was psychological. The doubt which had been seeping into the middle-class mind during the thirty years or so before 1914 was massively reinforced by the experience of 1914–1918. The war, begun as a great patriotic adventure to be carried swiftly to success in a matter of months, had turned into a four-year nightmare of slaughter, much of it apparently pointless. One of the casualties was the spirit which an Air Marshal of the 1939 War later called 'the proud, confident morale of pre-1914 Britain'. None of the old certainties – political, social, economic, moral or religious – could ever be taken for granted again.

Some of this war damage might have been made good if peace had brought prosperity, but it did not. After a brief and hectic boom lasting about 18 months, the economy collapsed in 1920–1921. The industries worst hit were the industries heavily dependent on world trade, and on which much of the prosperity of late-Victorian Britain had been based – cotton; coal; iron and steel; heavy engineering, especially shipbuilding. For a variety of reasons, none of these 'basic' industries, after 1921, ever got back to the pre-1914 level of prosperity. They were seriously depressed throughout the period between the two wars, casting a permanent shadow over the nation's life.

  * Newbolt's poem refers to a brass memorial in Clifton College Chapel to an officer who died young (*qui ante diem periit*). Presumably he was killed on the Indian frontier (*procul hinc* – far from here). But he was a soldier (*sed miles*), but he died for his country (*pro patria*).
  Dulce et decorum est pro patria mori – It is pleasant and fitting to die for one's country.

Afternoon Apron of White-spotted Muslin, with plain edge.
Price 5/11
Cap to match, with elastic at back.
Price 2/11

Afternoon Apron of White Muslin, trimmed tucks and embroidery.
Price 3/6
Cap with elastic back, trimmed embroidery and threaded black Velvet.
Price 1/11½

MAN-TAILORED COSTUME
Obtainable in a variety of the newest styles and materials.
To order.
From £7 7 0

SUITS FOR BUSINESS AND FORMAL WEAR

BLACK MORNING COAT

51 Men's clothes, 1929; women's, 1937.
52 (*Opposite*) 1929.

The economic and social results of chronic depression in the basic industries were concentrated in certain parts of the country and in certain groups in the community, notably cotton workers, miners and shipbuilders (unemployment among shipbuilders, between 1923 and 1938, never fell as low as 20 per cent and in 1932 it was 62 per cent). The psychological results spread wider. The basic industries were part of the framework of late Victorian Britain, closely identified in the public mind, especially the middle-class mind, with Imperial glory, world power, and social stability solidly based on industrial success. If the basic industries could not be put back in pre-war going order, what of the country and the Empire?

What indeed? From the Left came an answer: this is the failure of capitalism; this is the downfall, so long foretold, of the whole structure of private industry. More: capitalism, said voices on the Left, goes with imperialism: both belong to the same monstrous system of exploitation. If one goes, the other will go as well, and good riddance to both.

The middle classes in general, especially the middle-aged middle class, did not believe this explanation. They considered it wicked and dangerous. It was certainly too sweeping. Parts of the capitalist system were in decline, but that did not mean that capitalism was anywhere near collapse: simply that the British economy was going through fundamental changes, agonising and barely understood. As for

For British Cruises

British Frocks, etc. by Debenhams.

Debenham & Freebody
(Debenhams Limited)
WIGMORE STREET, LONDON, W.1.

exploitation of imperial territories, there was probably too little for the inhabitants' own good. Indian and colonial officials, by this stage in the history of the Empire, were devoted to the interests, as they saw them, of the people they had charge of, and by upbringing and education they were inclined to be suspicious of 'box wallahs' (businessmen), even the most exalted. They were not well qualified to encourage investment, and sometimes actively discouraged it.

It was difficult, nevertheless, to restore in the twenties and thirties anything like the robust optimism of the middle classes in their nineteenth century prime. Erosion of self-confidence went on as the young, especially, set about a thorough demolition job on their elders' objects of veneration. The Empire and the public schools were favourite targets. Pride in both began to give way to guilty doubt, at first only on the intellectual left, but spreading with the years to ever-widening circles. Lytton Strachey in *Eminent Victorians* (1918) attacked some of the great figures of the then recent past unfairly but wittily, and set a fashion for 'debunking'. 'Victorian' as an adjective began to take on overtones which it has never lost, though it has never wholly deserved them. 'Victorian' came to be associated with pomposity, stuffiness and repression, especially in sexual morals.

In 1933 renewed war with Germany began to be a serious, if still distant, possibility. The Union Society at Oxford, where the Left was strong, carried a motion 'that this House will in no circumstances fight for its king and country'. The motion was cunningly phrased to scandalize anyone over forty, which it did with most satisfying effect, at the same time obscuring the real issue: whether there was anything that the generation then aged 18–21 would fight for. In fact there was, as some showed in Spain within three or four years and many more on the battlefields of 1939–1945. Meanwhile the motion served to confirm the widespread impression that the nation was in a state of 'moral disarmament', and the length of young mens' hair was widely deplored.

53 Undergraduates at Cambridge 1935.

Intellectually and emotionally, between the two wars, the foundations of middle-class life were being undermined. Materially they were being strengthened. With depression went deflation, which meant that after the post-war boom collapsed, in 1920, prices fell, and they continued low in relation to salaries throughout the inter-war years, so that on £300 a year an unmarried man could live comfortably and run a car; on £500 a married man could raise a family; on £1,000 he was affluent. The average earnings of men in factories, in the twenties and thirties, seem to have been about £3 a week – well below the lowest range of salaries, which ran about £200 a year.

The central problem was to find a salary, or its equivalent in self-employment. This was never so easy before Hitler's war as it was in the lush years immediately after, but except in the years of acute crisis, 1920–1921 and 1931–1932, it may not have been quite so difficult as it has since been made to appear, and almost certainly much less difficult than at any time in the nineteenth century.

In the field of self-employment, although the basic industries were in decline, other industries were expanding, on the whole in fields which offered easier openings to starters and small men. To open a new shipyard before 1914 needed a great deal of capital. To buy a couple of ex-Army lorries in 1919 and start a transport service did not need much, and a good many ex-soldiers did it. Those who were tough and skilful enough to survive ferocious competition might do very well. Ship-building might be sick, but motor-car building was not, and although there could not be many William Morrises or Herbert Austins, there could be a great many garage and petrol-station owners, and there were. Building – a great

54 Fashion in motoring.

A PRACTICAL
MOTOR COAT

THE E. W. 4-SEATER SPORTS SALOON

on the New Wolseley "Hornet" Special Chassis.

many houses were built in the twenties and, especially, the thirties – was an activity, usually, for small or smallish firms. Inside the houses there were more electrical gadgets than ever before, and although, like cars, they would be made by large firms, they would be sold and serviced by small ones. So would radio sets, and by 1938 there was a set in 90 per cent of British households. To speak generally, the trend of the economy was away from the basic industries supplying export markets and towards industries supplying home demand, especially demand from private households. Manufacture was usually a matter for large companies with massive capital, but distribution and servicing gave scope for enterprise on a smaller scale: essentially the kind of enterprise which had always attracted middle-class talent, and still did.

The rise of large companies, between the wars, began to provide salaried employment, at last, on something like the scale which the Victorian middle classes had dreamt of but never achieved. The big firms needed clerks, typists, secretaries (at some point in these years men ceased to be secretaries, giving place entirely to women), and at every higher level, right up to the Board, managers. The demand was on a scale much greater than the old family networks could supply, even if families were still in control, and nepotism, in large companies, gave way to competitive selection. Some firms looked to the universities, particularly if they needed scientists, but in general British business felt it could get on without higher education and the universities, for their part, still considered Government service, at home or abroad, the Church, the professions and teaching to be the normal and proper occupations for graduates, with 'business' a rather eccentric and faintly discreditable minority choice.

Professional managers, generally speaking, were not wealthy men. They were usually far from being owners of the companies they worked for, and except by special and exceptional arrangement they usually had no direct interest in the profits. They were, in fact, much in the position of the hourly-paid workers on the factory floor, so far as the source of their income was concerned. It would be absurd, however, to suppose that the two groups saw matters in this way. The managers, by upbringing and habits of thought, were only too eager to assume the mantle of the owner-managers of the nineteenth century, with whom left-wing propagandists identified them. The result was a conflict between 'the two sides of industry' which, though less than half-real in its origins, was only too real in its results, since the working-class side was given every reason for believing that any improvement in the profitability of the firm was entirely to 'the bosses'' advantage and not at all to their own. 'Profit,' in many minds, came to mean much the same as 'greed' or 'theft', and notions of this sort were so relentlessly hammered home that even on the management side of the line feelings of uneasiness and guilt arose. This was unfortunate, seeing that without profit there could ultimately be no livelihood for either management or men. No doubt it was another manifestation of failing self-confidence.

'Professional status' was pursued as eagerly as ever, in the twenties and thirties, in occupations as diverse as advertising, cost accountancy, estate agency, radio engineering, work study and many more. The recognised professions of the nineteenth century and earlier – the law, medicine, the Church, engineering, architecture and perhaps one or two others – remained easily distinguishable, though it is difficult to draw up a definition of 'a profession' which covers them all. Outside them it became increasingly hard to say. exactly what requirements must be satisfied before an occupation could be dignified with the title of a profession, except that qualification by examination appeared to be one and the acceptance of some kind of ethical code another. Even then it was doubtful whether in public esteem, which was what mattered, many occupations outside the nineteenth century group were widely regarded as professions.

The older type of professional man – the lawyer, the doctor, the clergyman, the consulting engineer, the architect, the chartered accountant – was self-employed and was inclined to insist on his independence as an essential mark of professional standing. The newer professionals, or would-be professionals, tended to be specialists employed in government service, central or local, or in private industry. It was a tendency that accelerated as the demands of technology, administration and management became more complex. It raised problems, from time to time, for the professional conscience, but it added to opportunities for middle-class employment.

A middle-class man in mid-career, between the wars, might be earning £500–£600 a year. Senior civil servants would get two or three times that, and in business, at the upper levels, salaries might run a good deal higher, with perhaps bonuses or profit-sharing as well. High Court judges were paid £5,000, but that was much less than a successful barrister could earn (for work at very high pressure) and incomes at the very top of the largest companies could run to five figures, though the number of salaries at that level must have been very small indeed. Profits from private business, of course, could run from nothing to anything, but a successful man in small business might make an income of £2,000–£3,000 a year.

Income tax between the wars varied between 4s (20p) in the £ and 6s (30p), but the effective rate was much lower because income under £150 a year was exempt and above that level there was a range of lower rates and allowances which meant that a married man with two children paid no tax at all under £400 (earned) a year, and at that level only £1 13s 4d (£1.67). The working classes, broadly speaking, paid no income tax at all. The well-to-do, on the other hand, complained of the iniquity of it all. Most of them could remember the rates before the Great War – 1s 2d (6p) (rather high) in 1913–1914 – and on top of the standard rate, above £2,000 a year, there was surtax, rising ultimately to a rate of 7s 6d (37 p) in the £. A man with two children on £2,000 (earned) paid £327 10s (£327·50) tax in 1938, and that was considerably more than the total earnings of most men in the working class, who may not have felt that the boss's tax bill called for much sympathy.

75

DOLL'S HOUSE

DOLLS' HOUSE

ULTRA MODERN DOLL'S HOUSE

HORNBY TRAINS
& ROLLING STOCK

DOLLS' HOUSE

HORNBY No. 2 ELECTRIC TANK
LOCOMOTIVE (6-volt)

No. 2 SPECIAL TANK LOCOMOTIVE

FLAT TRUCK

HORNBY No. 1 Special PASSENGER TRAIN SET

55   Toys for middle class children reflect the standard of living, 1937.

The rich may have felt hard done by – they often said they did (you couldn't get servants) – but the general standard of middle-class life was rising. With mass production, cars became cheap, and before Hitler's war broke out you could get a *new* Ford for £100, and have change from 10s (50p) after filling the tank. That was a small car, but the price of a four-seater family saloon need not be more than £200–£300 unless you went in for the more expensive makes. At these prices, cars became a normal middle-class amenity. By the thirties speculative builders were providing quite small suburban houses with garages as a matter of course.

Houses themselves, usually hideous, were cheap, and by the thirties local authorities' regulations were strict enough to make sure that most of them were soundly built. £400, in the thirties, would house a family of four adequately, and £1,000, fairly spaciously. In the building boom of the thirties houses were being put up at a rate of 350,000 a year or so – a rate not reached again for twenty years and not exceeded until the sixties – and many of them were the work of speculative builders, testifying to the strength of middle-class demand and purchasing power in years when depression, in some parts of the country, was still deep.

Boarding-school education, in spite of the attacks on it, was still much prized by middle-class parents, and it might be essential if they had to live abroad. The usual course, for boys, was to send them to a preparatory school at about eight and on to a public school about five years later. At schools with any sort of a claim to be considered public schools, fees ran from £80 a year or less, through a large group at £100–£200, to a few at the top – Eton, Harrow, Winchester, one or two more – where fees were between £200 and £250. Fees for girls ran rather lower right through a similar scale.

A boarding school of some sort was thus within the reach of any moderately prosperous middle-class parent, and some who barely qualified for that description found the money somehow, though they might have done better to settle for a day school. Dayboy fees at the sort of schools discussed above rarely ran higher than £50 a year and they might be as low as £8, and again, for girls, the scale ran lower. Besides the public schools there were grammar schools, some independent, some grant-aided, and secondary schools entirely maintained by the counties, and beyond these again a large fringe of privately-owned schools, particularly for girls. Fees at all these schools, presumably, ran rather lower than those already quoted.

University education was not expensive outside Oxford and Cambridge, but at either of those bills would hardly be less than £250–£300 a year and could run as much higher as the undergraduate or his parents had means or inclination for. For bright boys, however, state and county scholarships, besides other awards, were fairly freely available, bringing the expense down a great deal. Nobody had the faintest premonition of the transformation that was to come over the whole conception of university education later in the century, and in most middle-class families it was still unusual, less because of the expense than because it hardly seemed necessary for more than a very few.

In the class structure of the country between the wars the upper middle class had become the effective upper class, with their fingers on most of the levers of power. The landed gentry – 'the county' – were still there, as they still are, and their social standing was unimpaired, but their wealth had been reduced by farming depression and estate duties and their political importance, in an industrial society, was small.

Social standing, even below the 'county' level, did not depend on wealth alone, or even chiefly, and indeed there was a tendency to despise the very rich whose position depended solely on their money. The upper middle class looked for a blend of upbringing, education, occupation and family connections associated with an outlook which, taking a fairly high degree of material well-being for granted, concentrated heavily on the notion of duty – duty to one's family, to one's profession, to the country, and to one's subordinates. The conception of duty might not always be enlightened, and from time to time it was betrayed, but there had been a marriage, in the middle-class mind, between the old upper-class notion of an inherited right to govern and the Puritanism of the old middle class, with its insistence on the importance of work and individual responsibility. The

56 Fire-side scene
(pre-television).

old aristocratic idea of a right to live in idleness, on the other hand, had been largely purged away, and so had the corresponding middle-class narrow-mindedness, concerned only with profit to the exclusion of wider considerations.

Lower down the scale, there was nothing like the same blending of different habits of mind. The working class, through hard experience, had come to put their faith in collectivism rather than in individual striving. Trade unions might and did compete with each other in seeking the collective advantage of their members, but within the union it was regarded simply as selfishness if one member competed with others to his own advantage. This cut across the whole middle-class ethic of self-help and individual responsibility, and no compromise was possible. The consequence was that an ambitious man from the working class who set out to 'better himself' would, simply by acting on that motive, cross the class barrier. He would be recognised, and probably approved of, within the middle class, as someone determined to 'get on'. By those whom he had grown up with, perhaps by his own family, he would very likely be regarded as a traitor to his class. In this conflict of outlook, far more than in differing material circumstances, lay the distinction between the middle class and the working class, and it was to become more important, rather than less, as the material circumstances of the two classes drew closer together after Hitler's war.

FURTHER READING

W. N. Medlicott, *Contemporary England 1914–1964*, 1967.

C. L. Mowat, *Britain between the Wars 1918–1940*, paperback edition 1968.

A. J. P. Taylor, *English History 1914–1945*, 1965.

Punch, bound volumes.

Edmund Blunden, *Undertones of War*, 1928.

Wilfred Owen, *Poems*, ed. Blunden, 1933.

7 Collapse . . . or Conquest?

During Hitler's war, in Great Britain, a powerful political attack was mounted against the social conditions of the twenties and thirties and against the reputation of the governments of those days, particularly the National Government which was in power from 1931 to 1940. The targets were not difficult to hit, particularly after failure in home policy was compounded by failure abroad. Stanley Baldwin and Neville Chamberlain, yesterday's heroes, were held up to public scorn, the public having conveniently forgotten its very recent overwhelming support for their policies.

Sir William Beveridge, in 1942, produced a report (*Social Insurance and Allied Services*) which proposed remedies for some of the leading causes of pre-war misery. It suggested comprehensive protection against want and sickness, includ-

57 Part of an advertisement which appeared in 1972 for the British United Provident Association, providing medical insurance schemes. In the age of the Welfare State, some people still prefer self-help.

ing a national health service and family allowances, all financed partly by 'stamps' and partly out of general taxation. The Beveridge Report rapidly became the gospel according to advanced liberal opinion. It was enthusiastically promoted, not least by the Army Bureau of Current Affairs, and it came to be accepted, by the mysterious processes of wartime thought, as symbolic of what the nation was fighting for, rather than against.

Churchill, Prime Minister in 1942, regarded social policy as a matter of small importance in wartime. There were other things to be seen to first and he had a healthy scepticism, born of experience last time, of promises about post-war conditions. He was not, however, actively obstructive, and the wartime coalition government endorsed Beveridge's proposals, which they linked with a public commitment to a policy of 'full employment', defined as a level of unemployment not higher than 3 per cent. Finally, again without the Prime Minister's enthusiasm, the Government laid the foundations of a post-war educational system dedicated to what were then considered, in some quarters with alarm, advanced egalitarian principles.

These were not socialist policies. Two of the figures most closely associated with them, Sir William Beveridge and R. A. Butler, were quintessential representatives of the new governing class, with connections by descent and by marriage among Indian civil servants, public-school headmasters, affluent owners of businesses, dons at Oxford and Cambridge, and among the upper-middle-class Establishment generally. They were men of first-class intellect, wide traditional culture, liberal principles. Perhaps men of this kind represented the finest flowering of the English middle classes – they would almost certainly have said they did – and there were many of them on all sides of politics and in the higher Civil Service. Let us look at their impact on one first-class measure of post-war social policy, the Education Act of 1944.

The educational system set up under the Act was based on the principle that children should be educated not according to their parents' wealth but according to their own ability, whatever that word might mean. Ability, for educational purposes, was to be defined and measured, just before the age of twelve, by a method of testing which quickly became known as 'the eleven-plus'. On the basis of the results of this test, with some possibility of later revision, children were to be selected for the kind of secondary school they were best fitted for. It seemed a sensible system, as well as a just one, and at first the establishment of the 'eleven-plus' test was regarded as triumph for progressive, egalitarian principles. Children were to get the education their natural ability fitted them for, and naturally the brightest would go furthest, to the jobs with the best pay and the highest social standing (not always found together), but that was not regarded as a drawback, except by those who regarded it as dangerously subversive of the social order. It was something that would have been highly approved of by Victorian radicals.

There were to be three main kinds of secondary school: 'Grammar Schools,'

58 School uniform.

'Secondary Modern Schools,' 'Secondary Technical Schools'. Only the first two were developed in large numbers, and they became at first the backbone of English secondary education, widely admired, and then, gradually, the centre of fierce controversy. From being the embodiment of progressive liberal wisdom they turned into symbols of class warfare, being increasingly represented as part of a plot to perpetuate the ascendancy of the middle class in capitalist society. Meanwhile alongside them, to the continuing outrage of left-wing opinion, the public schools continued to flourish in response to middle-class faith in their educational and social virtues.

The titles chosen for the two main types of secondary school – 'grammar schools' and 'secondary modern schools' – invite speculation about the unspoken, probably unconscious, assumptions underlying the Act. 'Grammar schools,' in the original meaning of the term, were schools set up, chiefly in the sixteenth and seventeenth centuries, to teach the grammar of Greek and Latin in preparation for advanced classical studies at Oxford or Cambridge, though many of their pupils stopped short of the university. In carrying out this function they came to enshrine a portion of the process of 'liberal education'* – that is, the education of a gentleman – which came to be admired and desired by the rising nineteenth century middle class. They were part of the educational tradition which culminated in the Victorian public schools, and so great was the prestige of these schools that the State secondary system, from its beginning in 1902, was modelled – often distantly – upon them.

* 'liberal' in this sense strictly means education fit for a free man. It has only a very distant connexion with the political application of the same word.

State secondary schools could never be public schools in the English sense (which, with good reason, never fails to astonish and confuse foreigners), but some of them could be the next best thing. They could be 'grammar schools', dispensing the equivalent of the old 'liberal education'. Hence the odd result that the schools intended to educate the bright children of the latter half of the twentieth century were named after schools originally designed for aspiring classical scholars of two or three centuries before. Moreover their top forms were generally called the Sixth Form, a title more closely associated with public school tradition than with logic. The choice of names, for schools and forms, strongly suggests a conservative cast of mind in those responsible for educational policy about 1944, even though their intentions were anything but conservative.

Much the same might be said of the naming of 'secondary modern schools', intended for those – the majority – whose ability, by 'eleven-plus' standards, did not fit them for grammar school education. In Victorian public schools the 'modern side' had been provided, by sceptical if benevolent headmasters, as a refuge for those who could not cope with the full rigour of the classics, and it is impossible to avoid the suspicion that something of this attitude lingered, no doubt subliminally, in the minds of those who framed the 1944 Act. Their intention, and we need not doubt their sincerity, was not to set up inferior schools for second-class citizens – simply different schools for different citizens – but, given the close link between grammar school education and occupations of good social standing, it was almost impossible to achieve for secondary modern schools anything like what the jargon of the day called 'parity of esteem' with the grammar schools. It was difficult to avoid drawing the conclusion, and the conclusion was widely drawn, especially by middle-class parents, that 'secondary modern' meant 'secondary worse'.

Beveridge, Butler and others of like mind were scarcely revolutionaries. Their purpose was not to overthrow the social order but to modify and strengthen it in the general tradition of English nineteenth century reform. Butler was a rising Conservative politician, and so was Harold Macmillan. Their party, adaptable as ever to the winds of change, quickly discovered virtue in conserving what soon came to be known as the Welfare State. Indeed they claimed it, not without a degree of truth (tempered by irony), as a Conservative invention.

This it may have been, but the Welfare State was largely brought into existence, after 1945, by Clement Attlee's Labour Governments. That in itself was enough to taint it, in minds less subtle than Butler's or Macmillan's, for Attlee's Governments were in theory devoted to socialist principles and in fact did pass important measures of nationalisation. No doubt private investors, having had several loss-makers taken off their hands for quite substantial compensation, should have been grateful, but instead they were confirmed in their suspicions that the whole package labelled *Welfare State* was part of a plot to undermine the moral fibre and economic strength of the nation.

In post-war social and economic policy, broadly agreed between the major

parties though much of it was, there was indeed a good deal to affront orthodox middle-class sentiment – particularly, perhaps, in provincial England, where the manoeuvres of the London mind have usually been regarded with grave suspicion. Why should the State, not content with outright nationalisation, insist on exerting far-reaching controls over 'the private sector'? Why not leave people to mind their own business? Wouldn't Beveridge's proposals, along with low unemployment, destroy the necessary incentives to individual effort and responsibility? What about the professional standing of the doctors, ensnared in the National Health Service? Where was all the money to come from? The answer to that was plain – from high taxation, chiefly on middle-class incomes.

But the confidence of the middle classes had been seriously weakened between the wars, and at the same time the long surge of middle-class conscience-power, building up since the 1880s and before, had played more destructively than ever on the foundations of the middle-class world. The 1945 Labour Government, identified in the orthodox middle-class mind with most of what it deplored in public policy, was nevertheless helped to its large majority (146) by a substantial middle-class vote, and at the head of the Government three senior Ministers – Attlee, Hugh Dalton, Sir Stafford Cripps – represented the upper middle class, the class of Butler and Macmillan, as it had evolved over the previous three-quarters of a century. So did many of the leading figures on the other side. The new middle class, continually reinforced from below *via* the grammar schools and the universities, seemed to be in almost as commanding a position in post-war British politics, left and right, as the landowners in the politics of the eighteenth century. And even the principal limitation on middle-class power had eighteenth-century undertones, for it was represented by the greatest borough-mongers since the days of George III: the Trade Unions with their sponsored Members.

On the Right of politics, or at any rate on the opposite side to the Labour Party, the Conservatives presented themselves as the champions of private capitalism and the opponents of State intervention in economic affairs. Historically, this was rather surprising, since in its origins Toryism had held commerce in contempt and had no objection in principle – indeed, much the reverse – to the exercise of authority by the State. But Toryism and Conservatism, though often lumped together, are by no means the same thing. Toryism is essentially an upper-class attitude: Conservatism is for the middle classes. What had happened, and had been happening for many years, was that one wing of the Liberal Party, representing the interests of private capitalism and what little remained of *laisser-faire* economics – both the concern of one large section of the middle class – had moved into Conservatism, in the process taking it over. The other Liberal wing, representing the English middle-class tradition of radical but not revolutionary change, had moved towards Labour, and perhaps also gone some way to taking over. In this way, it might be held, the triumph of nineteenth century Liberalism was complete, but at the cost of the effectiveness of the Liberal Party, which lingered in post-war Parliaments as a shrunken remnant held together by family ties and the memory, kept evergreen, of battles and betrayals long ago.

Post-war life in the United Kingdom turned out not at all as anyone expected. Economists, remembering 1919–1920, predicted a slump, and the wartime government took precautions. There was no need. World conditions, beyond the control of the British Government, carried material prosperity up, just as conditions in the thirties, equally uncontrollable, had depressed it. What government policy could do, and under both parties did do, was to impose high taxation, as in other advanced industrial countries, which channelled a good deal of the rising national wealth into social services, leaving plenty over for wage increases. The combined result was an unparalleled rise in working-class standards of living, symbolised by parking difficulties on council housing estates designed before anyone expected council tenants to own cars.

In the rising material prosperity since 1945 the middle classes have had their share. Full employment in private industry and the widening of government activity have produced far more salaried jobs than ever, and salaries have risen as

60 Employment for the middle classes – a London office block of the 1970s.

well as wages. Moreover there has not just been an increase at the lower end of the scale, producing a salaried proletariat. Low-paid clerical work of the old kind, indeed, has largely been transferred to machines, the machines being worked by girls on passage from school to marriage. The most attractive middle-class opportunities have presented themselves in large, complex companies, growing larger and yet more complex, and in the process requiring more and more managers and technologists, with good prospects of promotion in expanding businesses or of moving to other companies in search of better openings.

At the very top of the scale of industrial size are the multi-national corporations of the size and style of the great American oil and motor companies or, in Great Britain, Shell, Unilever and ICI. None of them, in their present form, is very old. They are new and conspicuous features of the social and industrial landscape. Their nature and purpose is not yet fully understood, either within themselves or outside. To say that they exist to make profits is true but insufficient, and to describe them as 'private enterprise' is misleading, since they represent a form of industrial organisation which is 'public' in every sense except nominal ownership by the State.

The managers of the large companies of the present day, nevertheless, are among the heirs of Victorian private enterprise. They act on the beliefs and assumptions of the Victorian middle classes, adapted rather uneasily to the circumstances of a later age. The profit motive, the classic driving force of Victorian business, is likely to be somewhat blunted for a salaried manager, though if his firm's results are really bad it will revive with a sudden sharp jab which may dislodge him from his job. The thoroughly Victorian belief in the virtue of individual ambition, of moving on always to better things, of keeping your eye on the job next or next but one ahead, is probably the strongest motive behind an able manager's career. It is not altogether a question of money. It is a question of self-respect, and as such it has its dark side. The man no longer moving up is likely to see himself as a failure, whether deservedly or not, and if he loses his job altogether the psychological results may be catastrophic even if the material consequences are not. In the nature of things, in salaried employment, the higher you go the fewer the possibilities of promotion are, and the manager who can go no further, even if he is doing a perfectly good job where he is, may suffer torments of frustration and jealousy which are not entirely out-weighed by a high salary, the firm's car and excellent pension arrangements. Nor are the miseries of blocked ambition peculiar to business life. They are the penalty, given a middle-class upbringing, of the expanded opportunities of salaried employment which the Victorian middle classes sought and which their descendants have found, but not yet learned to live with.

Woven into the pattern of rising prosperity there has been an expansion and a transformation of the communications industry. A literate but not highly educated population needs news and information, attractively conveyed. An affluent population wants entertainment. Mass marketing needs advertising. All these activities need media: printed, electronic, even live. The general style of communication, being addressed to the same audience, has increasingly been recognised as being similar in journalism, in entertainment, in advertising, and indeed the three are sometimes inextricably intertwined, so that people of similar talents can find employment on either side of the line or on both. They are apt to be young

61 The communications industry: the nine o'clock news, and BBC film unit in Vietnam.

men of high intelligence and good literary – not scientific – education, such as in times past would almost inevitably have gone into the Church and might have been very successful schoolmasters at the greater public schools.

The university is rapidly becoming the universal provider of trainee managers, technologists and scientists, to say nothing of accountants and lawyers, and the door to well-paid employment is becoming ever harder to pass without a degree or its equivalent. The conception of the proper function of a university has changed beyond recognition, and one result has been that graduates now tend to look upon jobs in business, either eagerly or with loathing, as normal rather than freakish. The academic industry itself has been one of the growth-points in the economy, and as it is a great consumer of its own product – graduates – it has added to the opportunities for middle-class employment.

Middle-class voices, since 1945, have often been heard complaining that a bright lad, starting from very little, can no longer make a fortune in the good old-fashioned way. The complaint is not borne out by the facts. A fortune is never easily made, but it has probably been less difficult to make one in the last twenty-five years than at any time in the past. World conditions and government policies, particularly the re-distribution of income by taxation, greatly deplored in middle-class circles, have combined to produce lively demand and rapid inflation. Anyone with the skill and daring to take advantage of the demand and keep ahead of the inflation has been able to do very well if he could borrow sufficient capital – not necessarily very much – to make a start. The middle classes have not lost their traditional eye for the main chance, and property development and finance have both been very rewarding in capital appreciation, while in the entertainment industry they have profited very handsomely from a very large demand. Taxation has certainly prevented the accumulation of capital from savings out of a salary, but how many middle-class heroes of the past ever grew

62   The London Stock Exchange.

rich in that way? Government policy with a mild left-wing tilt to it, it seems, is the best recipe in the world for successful private enterprise.

In the last quarter century more people than ever before have had a chance to move up in the world, partly through the general growth of opportunity described above and partly because it has been growing easier to get the education needed to make the most of the opportunity. Education is a great social escalator, carrying those who can climb on to the right part of it well above their origins, but although it makes movement across class barriers easier – for some – it does not remove the barriers themselves, and until very recently it has never been expected to, presumably because Englishmen, on the whole, have preferred liberty to equality, and it is difficult to have both.

Moving up is not comfortable. It is a strain for the individual, a strain for his family, a strain for the community. The process is not often rounded off in one lifetime. The complete middle-class man is one who has been born in middle-class surroundings and educated in middle-class ways. Even then, he may rebel, and he will be following well-established middle-class tradition if he does.

Moving up – competitive individualism – is the central principle of middle-class life and the mainspring of private capitalism, although businessmen frequently avoid or suppress competition if it seems sensible, as it often may be, to do so. Anyone who thinks he can make better terms for himself on his own, rather than relying on collective bargaining, belongs in sentiment to the middle class, and the tendency of a selective educational system, based on ability, is to produce people who feel like that, whatever class they were born in. Anyone of more than average ability, sharpened by several years of fierce competition at school and university, is unlikely to be content to merge his individual prospects with the prospects of a group, especially if he can see that a good many of the other members of the group are less able than himself.

63 Television in the classroom at a London comprehensive school.

The school system set up by the 1944 Education Act was geared to this machinery of personal achievement. It was designed to promote inequality, insofar as its central principle was selection according to ability. If we are ever to have a classless society, this sort of thing will never do, and it has fairly recently been discovered that one of the main aims of British politics is to produce a classless society. Accordingly, during the sixties, a campaign got under way to replace the system of 1944 with a 'comprehensive' system, in which the principle of selection according to ability is specifically rejected.

To minds brought up on traditional middle-class ways of thinking the argument that selection according to ability should be forbidden because it promotes inequality is not only wrong-headed but incomprehensible. Inequality is one of the facts of life and the middle classes, thank God, have less of it than most people. What are schools for if their brightest pupils, spotted as young as possible, are not to be trained to take the utmost advantage of their natural gifts? What is to happen to the nation if these natural gifts are not applied to the promotion of economic growth?

There is an escape hatch. You can buy your children out of State education altogether, which is what many middle-class parents do, thinking, as they pay the bills, that this is an altogether sensible and public-spirited thing to do, since it not only helps the children but it helps the country as well, by removing children from the overcrowded State system and training them to use their abilities in the most profitable way. Moreover it is the duty of parents, surely, to do their best for their children to the utmost their means will allow?

When fee-paying is attacked on principle, middle-class parents are both outraged and bewildered, since their most fundamental articles of belief are being challenged. On the other side, there arises a strong desire to harass fee-financed schools out of existence or, more straightforwardly, to make them illegal. On any showing, that would constitute a serious invasion of personal liberty, so here are the makings of a first-class political row.

The row about school fees is very much a row within the middle class. So too, perhaps, is the controversy about education generally. Under the Labour governments of the sixties it became very heated, because a determined attack on the grammar schools was opened and an assault on the public schools seemed likely. Then Labour were thrown out of office with their programme unfinished and the argument went off the boil.

It is certain to come to the boil again, because education, as a political issue, raises fundamental questions of social purpose and personal liberty. In doing so irreconcilable – indeed, mutually incomprehensible – systems of thought come into collision. Education is a matter of the deepest concern to the middle classes, who see it, quite rightly, as a key issue in the defence of their position. In more ebullient moods, they see it as an indispensable tool for the advancement of private capitalism, as well as the necessary preservative of a culture which they have been brought up to admire.

64 The start of the working day.

It is tempting to say that middle-class standing is a matter of outlook and that the test lies in acceptance or rejection of the principles of collective bargaining and group solidarity. This is true and it is fundamental, as the structure of British politics demonstrates, but it is not the whole truth.

Representative middle-class occupations, as a rule, bring much higher rewards than representative working-class occupations, so that the line between classes is a matter of occupation and income as well as outlook. Income determines what may be bought, including education, formal and informal. Thereby it goes a long way to govern tastes and the general style of an individual's or a family's life. Class differences come to be associated with the way people speak, eat, dress, make friends, vote and amuse themselves, with the districts they live in and even with the kind of church they go to. All of these, including the last, are likely to depend more or less heavily on their own or their parents' income, and therefore on the way the income is earned.

When all these matters are taken account of, an uneasy borderland begins to appear, through which it is impossible to plot a tidy frontier between classes. Most middle-class occupations include people of very varied social origins and correspondingly varied outlook. Some occupational groups which most people would assume to belong to the middle classes, including teachers and airline pilots, have accepted the tactics of collective bargaining, including strike action, and the professions have had their own version of them for a very long time. Some people in manual occupations earn more than clergymen and others who by general consent rank higher in the social scale. And where are we to put the police?

From considerations of this sort it follows that it is impossible to say quite how many middle-class people there are. Almost the only objective indicator is occupation, and on that basis a system of classification widely used in Great Britain places nearly 15m. people, not including children, in the middle classes, or about 35 per cent. of the adult population.* This may be an understatement of the number of people who by the test of general outlook would be found on the middle-class side of the fence. Voting at General Elections, whichever way the result goes, regularly shows a fairly even division of votes between the avowed party of the working class – Labour – and the party generally associated with middle-class ideas and interests – the Conservatives.

How, in a brief and general way, may 'middle-class ideas' be outlined at the present day? The starting-point is a belief in the value of competition as a spur to individual effort and in the virtue of individual effort itself. As a necessary consequence, the notion of personal inequality follows. People are not equal, and any attempt to make them so will lead to a lowering of standards and to tyranny.

    * Figures from *National Readership Survey*, June–December 1970.

66 Leisure in the 1970s: golf as a spectator sport.

Give every man a fair chance, by all means, but leave him alone, so far as possible, to gather the rewards of success, however he may define it for himself, or to endure the penalties of failure, and let the State provide a safety net rather than a feather bed for him to fall into, if fall he must.

Hard work and devotion to duty are highly regarded; pleasure, unless associated with strenuous physical effort, is suspect; leisure and idleness are inadmissible (how often is a businessman heard to admit having a moment to spare, in or out of the office?). Over all behaviour, especially sexual behaviour, there should be rigid self-control, and by the same token established authority should be respected, though respect for authority is compatible with a high regard for personal liberty, provided both sides keep to the rules.

A summary of this kind is bound to have an element of absurdity and caricature. No single individual is likely to hold all these views, and many are not peculiar to the middle classes. Moreover we are frequently assured that hypocrisy is the besetting sin of the respectable. Nevertheless something like this general pattern of thought – 'Puritanism', perhaps? – has a long historical association with the middle classes, and not in England only. If at present something approaching half our population – perhaps even the 'silent majority' of whom we hear so much – have been tinged (or tainted?) with it, then the middle-class bid for the mind has gone wide and deep and may be succeeding after all, in spite of the shocks and disillusionment of the last half-century.

Certainly middle-class views, associated as they quite rightly are with the whole system of private capitalism and industrialised society, have had enough life in them over the past ten years to provoke a world-wide storm of protest, relatively mild and urbane in Great Britain, very violent in the United States and elsewhere. Private capitalism, we are told, is irredeemably evil and the middle classes are the enemies of all good men.

Many of the leaders of protest come from the usual nursery of revolution: the middle classes. The middle classes in general, though shaken and puzzled by the fury of the onslaught, remain unconvinced of their own guilt and the moral rectitude of the other side. People in the middle classes can see as well as anyone else that there is a great deal wrong in the world. They can see also the inefficiencies, cruelties and absurdities of private capitalism serving – or manipulating – an acquisitive society. What they cannot see is that the alternatives, actual or proposed, are likely to be an improvement, and still less can they see that the destruction of 'the system' in a continuing revolution, without anything to put in its place, is likely to lead anywhere except to catastrophe.

Private capitalism, with all its faults, then begins to look like the most efficient and the most humane method of promoting economic growth so far demonstrated. Certainly in the past 150 years or so its results have been enormously greater than the results of any other system of economic organisation in history. Economic growth may not be altogether desirable, and the gloomier experts are prophesying that it may destroy us if one of several other disasters does not happen first. On the other hand it is quite certain that without economic growth a considerable proportion of the world's rising population will starve. Can the world afford to dispense with the economic growth which private capitalism has shown that it can provide? If not, can we afford to consign the middle classes and their way of life, in Great Britain or elsewhere, to the dustbin of the revolution?

FURTHER READING
Richard Hoggart, *The Uses of Literacy*, 1957.
Roy Lewis and Angus Maude, *The English Middle Classes*, 1949. *Professional People*, 1952.
Anthony Sampson, *The Anatomy of Britain Today*, 1965.
Picture Post 1938–50, ed. Tom Hopkinson, 1970.
Graham Turner, *The Leyland Papers*, 1971.

The Spiritual Railway

The Spiritual Railway
The Line to Heaven by Christ was made
With heavenly truth the Rails are laid.
From Earth to Heaven the Line extends
To Life Eternal where it ends.

Repentance is the Station then
Where Passengers are taken in.
No Fee for them is there to pay,
For Jesus is himself the way.

God's Word is the first Engineer
It points the way to Heaven so clear.
Through tunnels dark and dreary here
It does the way to Glory steer.

God's Love the Fire, his Truth the Steam,
Which drives the Engine and the Train.
All you who would to Glory ride,
Must come to Christ, in him abide.

In First, and Second, and Third Class,
Repentance, Faith and Holiness,
You must the way to Glory gain
Or you with Christ will not remain.

Come then poor Sinners, now's the time
At any Station on the Line,
If you'll repent and turn from sin
The Train will stop and take you in.

Epitaph to William Pickering, aged 30, and Richard Edger,
aged 24, who both died 24th December 1845.

Ely Cathedral Cloisters.

Index

Numbers in **bold type** refer to the illustrations